# THE KIDS ARE CRYING AGAIN

## AGAIN

### EMERGENCY COMMUNICATION SKILLS FOR PARTNERS AND PARENTS

ANNIE PESSKIN

# Contents

# Introduction

Falling in love is easy! But sustaining healthy relationships is hard. Being delighted by your kids is a cinch, coping with more hateful feelings towards them, harder.

I am aware that every relationship book you have ever opened basically says the same thing, namely, 'Communicate better!' But what does that *really* mean? And how do you actually *do* it?

I qualified as a psychotherapist a decade ago. From the hard work my patients have done in my consulting room, I have learnt a lot about the reasons *behind* the reasons that cause us to fight with our loved ones. These I share with you in the pages which follow. But understanding the *why* is only one half of the change process. The other half of changing is *how* to change.

This book is different to all others in this space because it offers you **exact words to say** in tricky arguments.

It might sound obvious but it is nonetheless true that good relationships make us happy and bad relationships make us sad.

A loving relationship has a greater bearing on how long we live than any other factor in our lives. It is far more significant than how much money we make or the things we can buy. **Connection** to a significant other (be they partner, child or friend) **confers immunity** from all manner of ills, from cancer to depression.

One reason relationships sour is that we stop believing the other person has got our interests at heart. If we don't feel they are fundamentally in our corner, we stop listening; if we stop listening, we stop trusting them; pretty soon, things fall apart. If kids are in this picture, this is an especially bad place to be.

Relationships are hard graft because we individually interpret reality and impose our expectations of what we are perceiving on to our partner/child. Our assumptions about what they are thinking, at any given moment, are an equally dangerous thing. Combine this with how little time we might spend trying to understand what *we* are feeling and the result is all too often a toxic cocktail of unhappiness and woe.

So this book makes the case for doing things **differently**. This is how it breaks down:

- *Part 1: You Do You* is all about getting to grips with yourself
- *Part 2: Firm Up the Foundations* explores the foundations of good communication, with exercises to improve your ability to listen and be listened to

- *Part 3: Time to Change* schools you in the art of negotiation providing exact phrases to use in difficult conversations
- *Part 4: When the Going Gets Tough* covers common pitfalls and how to avoid them
- *Part 5: Common Problems* offers some thoughts about frequent relationship difficulties and solutions to them
- *Part 6: Next Steps* is full of ways to find out more if you want to with signposts to future sources of help

I know reading words on a page is not same as sitting with me, an hour a week, in the comfort of my consulting room, with my attention focused solely on you and your story. I also know that putting our attention on how we feel is often a painful task – there is a reason my job involves boxes of tissues! But there is relief to be found from **working through** difficult feelings, rather than turning aside from them since they will only trip us up again and again, if we don't deal with them properly now.

When your feelings make you suffer, this book offers the tools to understand why you react the way you do, why you struggle to forgive and why you carry resentment around like stones in your backpack. My book also equips you with a whole raft of **new communication skills** to turn a fractious relationship into a nicer, happier one.

You can read it with your partner or you can read it alone. It makes sense to read it in order, but you can also just dip in and out, reading whatever page feels important to you in the moment.

A relationship is a shared undertaking and obviously, you can only be responsible for your half. Change is difficult.

But by using the techniques taught in this book, you can transform the way you relate to your loved one and therefore the way they relate to you. The result? **Fewer fights, more fun** and feeling <u>much</u> better!

Let your capacity for change AMAZE you!

# PART ONE

## YOU DO YOU

# Chapter 1

## Emotions

Emotions are foundational to our sense of ourselves and they play a key role in relationships by signalling to other people what we might be feeling at any given moment. They are like magnets, working to attract or repel another person, whether we realise it or not. For this reason, I thought it might be helpful to think about why we evolved them and how they can work, both with us and against us, in our relationships.

- **Who needs 'em?**
- **Jelly mould brains**
- **Emotions are the weather**
- **What are our emotional needs?**

### Who Needs 'Em?

Evolution stumbled upon emotions as an effective way to alert us to our needs and to help us find ways to get them met. Examples are a baby's inbuilt capacity to cry to bring a parent to them, or the joy all youngsters feel in rough-and-tumble play. **Emotions are conserved** in every generation because by and large they work to keep us safe, fed and able to attract a mate!

It is unfortunate that our first two evolutionary drives (to **survive** and **reproduce**) lead, in our particular species at any rate, to the following nasties: greed, selfishness, fear, anger, anxiety, envy, jealousy, disloyalty, resentment and a general aura of discontent when we don't get exactly what we want. I am sorry to say that all these nasty tendencies are built-in to me, you, your partner and your children as well as everyone else you know!

The third drive evolution bequeathed to mammals (to **care** and to **play**) is expressed to the *nth* degree in humans. This is because human babies are born *so* much more vulnerable and dependent than even our closest living relative, the chimpanzee. If a baby were born with its brain as well developed as a newborn chimp, they would stay in the womb for 20 months, not 9! Parenting very helpless babies was the trade-off our ancestors made for being able to walk on two legs, sometime around 2 million years ago. What's more, our brains are not fully developed until we are a whopping 25 years old. This means humans have had to develop very strong caring and sharing instincts to reproduce successfully.

Put simply, this means humans have a unique capacity for love. So to **thrive**, not just survive, we need to give and receive love on a daily basis. Our ruthless and self-serving aspects (which exist to enable us to survive and reproduce) can be tempered by this third, even **stronger** drive, to love and **connect**. But whether we can do this depends a great deal on how we were loved as little ones.

## JELLY MOULD BRAINS

I often say to patients that when we are born, our brains are like just-made jelly; the shape we end up as depends on the jelly mould we are poured into. The mould's shape is how we are treated by our caregivers as little ones. If lovingly cared for, our connections to others come easily and trust is a straightforward process. If we aren't, then making and maintaining relationships, empathising with loved ones ,or apologising when we get things wrong may prove more of a struggle.

So if you or your partner did not receive appropriate care as a child, perhaps because caregivers were neglectful, abusive, or both, then it is important to recognise that you and/or your partner's capacity to **connect** to each other and your children will be affected.

See the following sections for more on this: *Keeping calm (Part 1, Chapter 6), Difficult behaviours (Part 4, Chapter 24), Being blamed (Part 4, Chapter 23), Your anger (Part 1, Chapter 7), Misunderstandings (Part 4, Chapter 21), Violence (Part 4, Chapter 27), Self protection (Part 4, Chapter 28) and Anger with the world (Part 5, Chapter 34).*

## EMOTIONS ARE THE WEATHER

The other key thing I want to emphasise about emotions is that they are **bodily** events. When faced with an opportunity or a threat, emotions start in the brain but end in the body: blushing cheeks, gritted teeth, thumping hearts, shallow breathing, balled-up fists, crying eyes, sweaty palms, frowns, smiles etc..

This is because emotions bubble up from the part of the brain we still share with our mammalian cousins (the limbic system which wraps around and above the brain stem). Emotions exist and are expressed without and beyond words, in **facial expressions** and especially in **tone of voice**. We are always experiencing some emotion or other. Like the weather, we are sometimes stormy and sometimes enjoying blue skies; what is inevitable is that our emotions, like the weather, are always **changing**.

Long before you open your mouth to speak, your partner/child will have unconsciously picked up the bodily cues you are giving out about your emotional weather. And vice versa. This means even if you are not aware of your emotional state, they will be and your denial of a certain weather state will not wash with them. It is better to **get good at noticing** your emotions and trying to understand what has caused them, than to waste time denying them. They will not be fooled and neither are you when it happens the other way around!

## WHAT ARE OUR EMOTIONAL NEEDS?

So if emotions evolved to help us meet our needs, it might be useful to recap on just what emotions are good to feel on a regular basis.

The list below comes from The Center for Nonviolent Communication (www.cnvc.org). As you read it, draw a circle round, or highlight with your e-reader, how many of your needs can only be met by others. This is why cultivating happier relationships in your life makes so much sense.

## CONNECTION

Acceptance, affection, appreciation, belonging, cooperation, communication, community, companionship, compassion, consideration, consistency, empathy, inclusion, love, mutuality, intimacy nurturing, respect/self-respect, safety, security, stability, support, to know and be known, to see and be seen, to understand and be understood, trust, warmth

## PHYSICAL WELL-BEING

Air, food, movement/exercise, rest/sleep, sexual expression, safety, shelter, touch, water

## HONESTY

Authenticity, integrity, presence

## PLAY

Joy, humour

## PEACE

Beauty, communion, ease, equality, harmony, inspiration, order

## AUTONOMY

Choice, freedom, independence, space, spontaneity

## MEANING

Awareness, celebration of life, challenge, clarity, competence, consciousness, contribution, creativity, discovery, efficacy, effectiveness, growth, hope, learning, mourning, participation, purpose, self-expression, stimulation, to matter, understanding.

For how to **get our needs met**, see the next chapter on *Feelings*.

# Chapter 2

---

## Feelings

What is the difference between an emotion and a feeling? Why does it matter? In this section, I explain how communication of an emotion turns it into a feeling and how a failure to identify how we feel can block our capacity to solve all manner of relationship difficulties.

- **How do you feel?**
- **What do you feel?**
- **How it feels when your needs are met**
- **How it feels when you are needs are not met**
- **SIFTing your feelings**
- **Changing your relationship**

## How Do You Feel?

Oddly enough, emotions only become **feelings** when someone else bothers to label what we are experiencing with a name. Then the emotion exists as a word that links us to someone else: 'You seem *anxious*, are you?' **Feelings are** always about **connection** to others, either in the moment ('I

can't believe you have left your toothbrush in the sink <u>again</u>!'
- *anger*) or to do with experiences in the past ('I wake up some
mornings and just feel really blue' - *sadness*).

If we were lucky, between birth and aged 3, we had an
attentive and thoughtful caregiver who did a good job of
labelling our emotional weather.

To give an example, imagine your toddler self falling over
and starting to cry. Your caregiver hopefully came over and
said, "Oh poor you, you just fell over that truck and hurt
your foot. Oh no! There is blood on your knee! Let me kiss it
better for you". The words and actions from your caregiver
on noticing you were hurt did two important things for your
molten jelly brain.

They signified that a) someone **loved** you and b) someone
was **connected** to what you were experiencing. This made
you feel **safe** to move through the emotional storm into
bluer skies because the physical pain of falling was made
better by your caregiver's kindness and affection which was
communicated via a sympathetic tone of voice and helpful
actions ('Poor you', a cuddle and a plaster).

But what if our caregiver didn't notice we fell over? Perhaps
when we brought our bloody knee to them, they shouted at
us for interrupting their TV programme. Instead of feeling
helped to cope with the physical pain of falling, our jelly
brain learnt something else, namely '**You are alone**'. No-
one put into language what we felt, no nurturing action
resulted and no connection to our caregiver was felt.

If this happened too often to us as a young one, we may well
grow up to have great difficulty using language, or indeed
rational thought, to understand what is driving our emotions.
This is because we didn't get to *learn* about our feelings from

our caregiver, but instead, we simply *experienced* our emotions as physical events in our body.

We didn't get experiences with labels as that only comes when another person interprets through facial expression, tone of voice and language what we are experiencing. Instead, we got an **emotional overwhelm** of unbearable intensity.

If this sounds familiar, then you/your partner may also have trouble trusting other people or empathising with their problems. When we were little, no-one interpreted how we felt and as a result, now we are older, we commonly lose our tempers easily, lash out verbally or physically, and/or hurt ourselves when we feel overwhelmed.

But by learning how to label and manage our nastier emotions (fear, anger, selfishness, blaming, resentment), we can turn emotions into words (ie. communicate our **feelings**).

When we have **learnt to communicate** what we are feeling, we can use our partner to help us feel loved and connected (just as our caregiver should have done for us when we were little). Then, in turn, our relationships can become an oasis of calm; a place of mutual respect, tolerance and diplomacy.

If we can help ourselves slow down and analyse what is happening in our body when in the grip of powerful emotions, we can learn to communicate our feelings. This is the first step to escape unhelpful cycles of destructive arguing.

See *Keeping calm (Part 1, Chapter 6)* for more on this.

## WHAT DO YOU FEEL?

If we go to the doctor, the first thing they usually ask is, 'What is the matter?' By describing our symptoms, the doctor figures out what is wrong with us.

People come to see me because they **suffering** not **from** physical pain per se, but from their **feelings**. When they arrive, they often don't know why, but by using my trained ear, my job is to help them make sense of why they feel what they feel.

For example, someone might come in saying, 'I feel useless, I can't cope with work, I can't find a partner'. After many sessions, together we build up a picture of how they felt when they were little. We discover their father was incredibly critical and their mother never stood up to him.

They often felt alone with their problems and were afraid to ask for help for fear it would bring more criticism. This is the 'mould' their jelly brain was poured into, so of course they feel 'useless', though in fact the *actual* problem is how profoundly they **mistrust** others and therefore can't tolerate any relationship for very long.

## HOW IT FEELS WHEN YOUR NEEDS ARE MET

The words below express a combination of emotional states and physical sensations. The list is neither exhaustive nor definitive but it is a starting place to engage in a process of deepening self-discovery and to facilitate greater understanding and connection. (This list is taken from The Center for Nonviolent Communication, www.cnvc.org, copyright 2005).

Please highlight the feelings you would like to **feel more** regularly in your relationship:

## AFFECTIONATE
Compassionate, friendly, loving, open-hearted, sympathetic, tender, warm

## ENGAGED
Absorbed, alert, curious, engrossed, enchanted, entranced, fascinated, interested, intrigued, involved, spellbound, stimulated

## HOPEFUL
Expectant, encouraged, optimistic

## CONFIDENT
Empowered, open, proud, safe, secure

## EXCITED
Amazed, animated, ardent, aroused, astonished, dazzled, eager, energetic, enthusiastic, giddy, invigorated, lively, passionate, surprised, vibrant

## GRATEFUL
Appreciative, moved, thankful, touched

## INSPIRED
Amazed, awed, wonder

## JOYFUL
Amused, delighted, glad, happy, jubilant, pleased, tickled

## EXHILARATED

Blissful, ecstatic, elated, enthralled, exuberant, radiant, rapturous, thrilled

## PEACEFUL

Calm, clear-headed, comfortable, centered, content, equanimous, fulfilled, mellow, quiet, relaxed, relieved, satisfied, serene, still, tranquil, trusting

## REFRESHED

Enlivened, rejuvenated, renewed, rested, restored, revived

## How It Feels When Your Needs Are Not Met

So, you know what you want to feel more of. But what do you want to **feel less** of? The following list describes how we feel when our needs are not being met. (This list is taken from The Center for Nonviolent Communication, www.cnvc.org, copyright 2005).

Highlight the feelings you wish you didn't experience in your relationship:

## AFRAID

Apprehensive, dread, foreboding, frightened, mistrustful, panicked, petrified, scared, suspicious, terrified, wary, worried

## ANNOYED

Aggravated, dismayed, disgruntled, displeased, exasperated, frustrated, impatient, irritated, irked

## ANGRY
Enraged, furious, incensed, indignant, irate, livid, outraged, resentful

## AVERSION
Animosity, appalled, contempt, disgusted, dislike, hate, horrified, hostile, repulsed

## CONFUSED
Ambivalent, baffled, bewildered, dazed, hesitant, lost, mystified, perplexed, puzzled, torn

## DISCONNECTED
Alienated, aloof, apathetic, bored, cold, detached, distant, distracted, indifferent, numb, removed, uninterested, withdrawn

## DISQUIET
Agitated, alarmed, discombobulated, disconcerted, disturbed, perturbed, rattled, restless, shocked, startled, surprised, troubled, turbulent, turmoil, uncomfortable, uneasy, unnerved, unsettled, upset

## EMBARRASSED
Ashamed, chagrined, flustered, guilty, mortified, self-conscious

## FATIGUE
Beat, burnt out, depleted, exhausted, lethargic, listless, sleepy, tired, weary, worn out

## PAIN
Agony, anguished, bereaved, devastated, grief, heartbroken, hurt, lonely, miserable, regretful, remorseful

## SAD

Depressed, dejected, despair, despondent, disappointed, discouraged, disheartened, forlorn, gloomy, heavy-hearted, hopeless, melancholy, unhappy, wretched

## TENSE

Anxious, cranky, distressed, distraught, edgy, fidgety, frazzled, irritable, jittery, nervous, overwhelmed, restless, stressed out

## VULNERABLE

Fragile, guarded, helpless, insecure, leery, reserved, sensitive, shaky

## YEARNING

Envious, jealous, longing, nostalgic, pining, wistful

## SIFT-ING YOUR FEELINGS

You might not initially be very good at knowing exactly what you feel. Using Dr. Daniel Siegel's method of SIFT-ing is an excellent way to improve your 'read' of what is going on inside you.

**S - Sensations** – what are you feeling, how intensely and where are you feeling it in your body?

**I - Images** – what are you imagining you could do to your partner/child while in the grip of these sensations?

**F - Feelings** – can you get a name to the sensations/images you are experiencing? Anger? Shame? Fury? Rage? Frustration? Jealousy? Fear?

**T – Thoughts** – can you get any words to what you are feeling? Can you practice saying what you are feeling as calmly and as thoughtfully as you can, first to yourself in the mirror, then to your partner/child?

## Changing Your Relationship

### **Worksheet 1 - Feelings You Don't Want to Feel**

This worksheet is designed to help you identify exactly what kinds of feelings you are suffering from. Copy this out and fill it in using pencil and paper. The act of physically writing down each feeling will help you figure out what you feel, where you feel it in your body and how often.

I suggest filling out this worksheet whenever you are struggling with your feelings, so you can confidently identify what feelings are difficult for you right now. You can only work on something you can name, after all.

For help on processing these feelings, see *Keeping calm (Part 1, Chapter 6)*.

### **Worksheet 2 - Fixing Your Relationship**

This worksheet diagnoses what problems you want to fix in your relationship.

If your partner is on board at this stage, they can fill out both worksheets for themselves while you do yours. But don't share them with each other yet.

Give yourself 10 minutes of quiet time to see what occurs to you and write it down. The act of writing gives your brain time to reflect so definitely set a timer and use a pen and paper.

Don't edit yourself – whatever comes to mind is valid, no matter how big or small. If things occur later on you want to add, then don't be afraid to keep adding items.

The completed worksheets 1 & 2 will have given you a list of 'symptoms' you want to cure so you can prioritise which conversations to have first.

## Worksheet 3 - Goals for Change

Now you have filled in Worksheet 3, you will have a clearer idea of what you want to change in your relationship and hopefully your partner will have their own Worksheet 3 filled in too.

The next chapter on *Thinking* will help you navigate the negotiations that lie ahead in turning your Goals for Change (Worksheet 3) into reality.

## Worksheet One

# Feelings You Don't Want to Feel

| What you wish you didn't feel | Where in your body you feel it | How often per week you feel it | Can you spot the trigger? |
|---|---|---|---|
| Anxious | Around my heart | Every day | When I think about money |
| | | | |
| | | | |
| | | | |
| | | | |
| | | | |
| | | | |
| | | | |
| | | | |
| | | | |
| | | | |
| | | | |

## Worksheet Two

# Your Relationship

| What you want to feel more of | What you could change to feel it |
| --- | --- |
| Understood | Less phone time |
| | |
| | |
| | |
| | |
| | |
| | |
| | |
| | |

## Worksheet Three

# Your Goals for Change

| Your feelings | What you need | What you want to change in your relationship |
|---|---|---|
| Loneliness | More physical contact | How often you cuddle up together |
| | | |
| | | |
| | | |
| | | |
| | | |
| | | |
| | | |

# Chapter 3

## Thinking

You might think something as automatic as thinking is simple. Alas it is not, for at least 95% our thinking is unconscious and this leads us to behave in ways we didn't apparently choose, with consequences we definitely didn't want!

What follows are some useful things to have up your sleeve as you relate to your partner/child and try to meet your own needs within the relationship.

- **Change is possible**
- **Choice confuses**
- **Framing and context**
- **The mind is its own place**
- **Is and oughts**

### Change Is Possible

Look at how fast children grow. Go out into nature and notice how nature is constantly in flux.

One of the exciting things about modern life is that we know so much more about our brains. We now know that brains change according to what we do with them; e.g. a particular part of London taxi drivers' brains (the hippocampus) grows larger, the more streets they learn to navigate. Brains can change. This is why if we start a new sport and keep on doing it, of course we get better at it! This is good news for our capacity to change!

But there is a problem.

Modern neuroscience has discovered that our brain is a *giant prediction machine*, for more on this see *Other Resources (Part 6, Chapter 39)*. This means it is not that our brains 'read' the outside and reproduce it for us on the inside. Instead, we unconsciously **generate a prediction** of what any given moment is like *based on our past experience* and then we use information flowing from the outside (from our eyes, ears, smell etc.) to *verify* what we have predicted.

This means the **stories** you tell yourself really **matter**. If you were parented by abusive, hostile, anxious or irresponsible caregivers, you may well have learned to tell yourself, 'Oh, I could never do that. That's too hard'.

But as a child you learnt to read, for example, because you are reading this right now. Meanwhile your childrens' brains are super jelly-like right now, primed to learn from *you* and everyone around them. Modern neuroscience has shown that our brains keep growing new connections every single day of our lives, even until we are 100, a feature scientists term neuroplasticity.

Crucially, this means we are **never too old** to learn how to do something. Indeed if we feed the brain with stimulation by practicing new things – take up tango, learn German, practice tai chi - the ageing process slows down. The old adage, 'Use it or lose it' really is true.

And it applies just as much to our ability to love.

But something precedes the capacity to learn a new skill and that is the belief you start with – 'I *can* versus I *cannot*'.

Since we are talking about improving relationships in this book, **learning something together** is what matters. Having fun together is a key step on the path to happier relating.

Believe it or not, fun has measurable effects on your future happiness. For more on this, see Laughter *(Part 2, Chapter 10)* and look up the links on *Laughter* in *Other Resources (Part 6, Chapter 39)*.

In summary then:

- tell your infantile, bullying, inner voice that you can do new things
- find a new activity and start doing it together
- remember you are never too old to change, **neuroplastic is you!**

I want to encourage you to challenge unhelpful thoughts and replace them with other possibilities. Here are some examples to help:

**Example 1:** *"I feel frightened. All dogs are dangerous. Some dogs are dangerous. That dog right in front of me is wagging its tail and its owner has it on a lead."*

<u>Analysis:</u> In the example above, the idea that 'Xs' (dogs) are *always* 'Y' (dangerous) is a very common, unchallenged

prediction. Closer attention to detail can change your stress level.

Notice how the thoughts can change from 'All Xs are always Y' to 'Some Xs are *sometimes* 'Y'. This is a preferable mind set requiring you to ask yourself: 'What is the present **evidence** I can use to determine whether this particular dog is dangerous?'

**Example 2:** *"I feel hurt. My partner must know I feel hurt."*

<u>Analysis</u>: I wonder if my partner realises I feel hurt? Perhaps my partner has good reason for doing what they did. Is my partner a mind-reader? Am I mind-reading their intentions? Why don't I ask, check, clarify?

**Example 3:** *"I've always done it this way so it must* be the best way to do it and I must insist it is done this way."

<u>Analysis:</u> Travel documentaries on TV teach us that foreigners cook food differently, dance differently, believe different things. So perhaps there *are* other ways to do things. Perhaps if I began my communication with 'Let's **try** X' rather than 'You *must* do Y' my partner/child might feel less annoyed by what they experience as my controlling behaviour.

**Example 4:** *"If X doesn't happen, catastrophe will follow"*.

<u>Analysis:</u> It is useful to understand that **risk exists in two parts**. Part 1 is the possibility of something happening; and Part 2 is the consequences of it happening. Quite often we create a lot of fear and stress by over-emphasising Part 1 (the possibility) and forgetting Part 2 (the consequences) at our peril.

Fear of flying is a good example of this, where we over-emphasise the *consequences* of crashing while under-emphasising the incredible unlikeliness of the *possibility* of a crash occurring, since in actual fact, you are far more likely to die in a motorway accident than on an aeroplane.

**Example 5:** One group of patients (Group 1) were told an operation had a 70% record of success, A second group (Group 2) were told there was a 30% chance of failure. Many of Group 1 went ahead with the procedure; very few in Group 2 went ahead. The information supplied was identical, only the **framing** of percentages was different.

Analysis: The lesson here is challenge your framing!

**Now can you practice?**

Write down any "truth claim'" you are faced with, whether it's your own or another's. Ask yourself:-

- Is it true, why is it true, what habit of mine assumes it is true, is the evidence reliable?
- How am I framing this, in what context?
- What alternative interpretations are possible? What do others think and why?
- If I act and am wrong, what do I lose? Money, face, status? Does it matter?
- What is my plan B?

See *The Art of Negotiation (Part 3, Chapter 17)* for more on this.

## CHOICE CONFUSES

For most of our existence as Homo sapiens, we've had very few choices. Before washing machines, combine harvesters and contraception (!) there was little free time, little disposable income and little consumer choice. In a village, there might be only three possible marriage partners (the one with the limp, the one with the spots, the one with the bad temper!) Having few choices and little advertising to make us feel like we were lacking stuff, we accepted the restricted, limited choices life presented. How times have changed! How many yoghurt products were you assaulted by on your last visit to the supermarket?

Psychology science has established the fact that our brains are confused by choice. Barry Schwartz has done some good science on this (see *Other Resources - Part 6, Chapter 39*) and has shown that too much choice leads to confusion. Did I make the right choice? This experience is known as 'Buyer's Remorse' and has been shown to depress your mood.

It is sad to say that product marketing is deliberately designed to confuse you so that your unconscious cues take over. You choose the 'deluxe' option to reinforce fragile self-esteem ('You're worth it!'). You fall for the BOGOF (buy-one-get-one-free) because it seemed like a bargain but feel bad when you end up throwing away the second item. Or you are nudged into making a rash decision by 'Hurry – Offer Ends Soon'.

So what can you do in the face of powerful advertising cues? Decide what your primary aim is for every decision you need to make. Take yoghurt as an example. Is it protein, fat or sugar you care about most? If you decide in advance what is most important to you, then choices in the moment that work for *you* are easier to make.

## FRAMING AND CONTEXT

Our opinions, judgements and actions are not stable. We are heavily influenced by how unconscious cues affect us and they include all **non-verbal cues** especially facial

expression, tone of voice and body language. See
*Communicating Well (Part 2, Chapter 12)* for more on this.

Retail shops control their lighting, pay special companies to
select their music playlists, think carefully about even the
aromas they release. Rather than be a victim of their tricks,
why not use the science behind their insights to learn to talk
so your partner will listen?

For example, think about how it feels to your partner to
return home of an evening. What do they see? A messy
kitchen, toys all over the floor? What do they hear? You,
shouting at the kids? What do they smell? Dirty nappies, a
badly-ventilated room?

What if you lit a nice smelly candle, aired the room and
bothered to go and greet them in the hall with a smile and a
hug as they came in, no matter how wrung out and
exhausted you felt by the demands of your routine domestic
heroism?

If your habit is to scowl at them resentfully when they come
into the kitchen rather than say 'Hi', it *may well be* exactly
what you are feeling! But what is the message they are
getting? If you realise you have the power to cultivate in
them a feeling that coming home to share their life with *you* is
an instant relief from the hassles of their life in the wider
world, then you are immediately transforming your
relationship from a place of conflict into something
resembling a sanctuary.


## THE MIND IS ITS OWN PLACE

Read these 'sentences':

- Tte erth is fla.

- Dois a d c a t s ften h ve fl e e

The letters are meaningless, right? But your brain predicts the letters assembled on the page 'should' make meaning. So without any conscious effort, your brain will have replaced, added and reshuffled the letters to make commonplace observations: 'The earth is flat' and 'Dogs and cats often have fleas'.

What this simple example reveals are **four** important lessons:

1. We individually interpret **reality**.
2. We impose our **predictions** on what we sense and call it 'knowing'.
3. The future is full of possibilities and probabilities, **not certainties**.
4. If we **adjust** our expectations to accept uncertainty, life is much less stressful.

## Is and Oughts

We know the brain uses **shortcuts** to conserve energy and that memory stores the 'new' in easily accessible places. The new is recognised by comparing it to the known. Faced with new data, we seize upon that which confirms our pre-existing opinions as this *feels* nicer for us. This is one example of what is known as *cognitive bias*. For more on this see **Cognitive Bias** in *Other Resources (Part 6, Chapter 39)*.

If you do know about it, then it might be time to examine which cognitive biases you currently suffer from. A way to do this is to recognise another shortcut employed by our labour-saving brain, which is to confuse an "is" with an "ought"'.

We humans find it all-too-easy to build arguments on familiar but false assumptions. For example, you might observe that: 'Some dogs and some children are disobedient'. But it is easy, for one's own convenience, to invent the "ought" that, 'Dogs and children *should* be obedient' and, 'Therefore my dog or child *must* be obedient'.

We rarely bother, or are capable of defining, exactly *what* we mean by 'obedient'. Yet we find that when our child or dog are *not* obedient at any particular time, we get upset and angry. Anger is not helpful because it causes the brain chemical cortisol to be released and this essentially shuts off thinking. See *Violence (Part 4, Chapter 27)* and *Coping with Teenagers (Part 5, Chapter 35)* for more on this. This can lead to inappropriate and unhelpful reactions to the 'disobedient' dog or child.

The point is this: many of us live in a fury of comparing what observably 'is' with what we personally think 'ought' to be the case. So let's revisit the "oughts" which can so upset us. Whose "oughts" are they? Your grandmother's? Your best friend's? Society's norms? Have you actually discussed and agreed with your partner or child the norm which undergirds your opinion on something which annoys you? Or is it just your own personal preferences based on an unexamined mish-mash of all the above?

Before making demands on the world, be they on your partner, your child, or even your dog, check your fundamental assumptions. Just because you *feel* something is true or right, and therefore *ought* to happen at your whim, I hope you can see how unhelpful this is.

Think about two opinions you currently hold which you can see are not facts. Examples might be 'My child should have a tidy room', or 'My partner should like my family'. Recognise these are *your* opinions. Therefore of course they are important to *you*. By all means, discuss them with your child and your partner, but do not expect the other person to agree with your *opinion* as though it were a *fact*.

When we calm down, get organised and learn to think better, life can become much less fractious and a lot more fun.

## A TAKEAWAY

HAPPINESS = REALITY minus EXPECTATIONS

- Your actions are based on your own (often unconscious) assumptions, beliefs, predictions and expectations.
- Don't be surprised if your non-negotiated 'oughts' conflict with other people's 'oughts' - especially those of your partner or child!
- If you grasp that your opinions are not facts then sharing, compromising and living together becomes much easier. Better to bend than break.

# Chapter 4

## Expectations

Hinduism's equivalent of the Bible, the Bhaghavad Gita, says, 'Happiness begins where expectations end'. This chapter helps you think about how the expectations you may unthinkingly be putting on your relationship may be a source of unhappiness for you both.

- **What to expect**
- **Role models**

### What To Expect

Have you ever interrogated your own expectations when it comes to your relationship? When we do this, we can often be surprised by what we find. Obviously, we don't expect our partner to be fascinating, attentive and adoring ALL the time! Everyone is allowed a bad day, perhaps because they are feeling ill or low, due to things not going so well in their life. And we all know how being hungry or tired can make all of us quicker to anger. My husband calls hunger-fuelled anger, 'h-anger'!

But how frequently do you pull focus and ask yourself whether your partner is meeting your expectations and if not, why not? All too often, we get caught up in the humdrum and forget to ask the important questions, like 'Has this person done something or said something kind to me today? Have I done the same for them?' Or, 'Did my partner make me feel better about something I am troubled by this week and have I done the same for them?' Or, more pertinently, 'Have I asked them what might be troubling them this week?' And, 'Have they asked me?'

Study in detail the words on Worksheet 4:

# Worksheet Four

| LIST A | LIST B | LIST C |
|---|---|---|
| idolise | attachment to | |
| adore | admiration of | |
| enchanted by | respect for | |
| infatuated with | compassion for | |
| hankering after | tenderness towards | |
| think the world of | yearning for | |
| cherish | mad about | |
| crazy about | doting on | |
| passionate about | treasure | |
| besotted with | delight in | |
| lust for | devoted to | |

I think if you are honest with yourself, you will recognise that the feelings you had for your partner at the start of your love affair would cluster in List A and that over time, you find yourself feeling more of the things in List B. Fill in your own current feelings about your partner in List C. This might include things from both Lists A and B.

Please consider the following questions:-

- Have your own expectations of your relationship changed since you met your partner?
- Have your circumstances changed?
- Which of those love words in the table above do you expect your partner to feel for you now? Take a pen and write them down.

Could you ask your partner to have a look at List A and B and write down what they feel for you in their own List C (on a good day)?

## ROLE MODELS

On whom do you base your expectations of relationships?

Family, friends, parents, neighbours, novels, films, TV soap operas, Facebook posts of happy families, InstaInfluencers?

Who are your role models for good relationships? Which couples do you actually know in real life whose relationships you admire? What is it you admire about them? Write down some of the key qualities you have observed. Eg. "I notice Peter always kisses Mary goodbye when they part from each other and I like that", or "I like the fact that Ben finds Amy really funny and they seem to enjoy a laugh together."

The most important influences on the relationship you make are the relationships you observed growing up - parents, step-parents, grandparents, aunts/uncles, friends' parents etc.).

What characteristics can you observe which are similar between their relationships and your own? Can you share your observations with your partner? What have they observed about those relationships? Can they see similarities between you and them? If so, what?

It is usually fine for *you* to slag off your family of origin, but you get defensive if someone else does, so remember the same applies to them!

As an outsider to your family of origin, your partner will likely have plenty of interesting things to say about this. Let them share their insights and then ask them if they would like to hear your observations about the relationships in their family of origin. But be sure you back up your observations with examples, so they don't feel like you are simply taking a generalised swipe at their family of origin!

## Chapter 5

# Improving Self-Esteem

We can often feel badly about ourselves and then make an assumption that our partner must see us the same way. This can cause many difficulties in relationships.

For example, it can lead us to demand reassurance from our partner, then disbelieve it when they give it. Imagine the couple who are getting ready to go out for an evening. She says, 'Do I look fat in this?' He replies, 'No, you look great.' She hears impatience in his voice and retorts, 'You're just saying that so we won't be late!' He ends up feeling unheard and cross.

So this chapter is about finding ways to separate how you experience yourself from how your partner *might* be experiencing you. It is so important to remember that you **cannot read** your partner's mind, however certain you feel you are. Uncertainty is your friend when it comes to relating to others.

- **Master your story**
- **Catch nasty thoughts**

- **Boost that gratitude practice**

## MASTER YOUR STORY

What makes human beings so very different from our closest cousins, chimpanzees? Our capacity to talk. What do we use our talking for? To tell stories of course. What defines a culture? Its set of shared stories. What defines your personal reality? The stories you tell yourself.

The idea of contentment probably sounds rather quaint! But the tales you tell yourself about your life really matter. They have the biggest impact in determining whether or not you feel contented. When we are stuck in 'self-ing', we are usually trapped in the unholy trinity of self-absorption, self-isolation and self-criticism.

A mindfulness practice quickly reveals that we have no 'self' as such, just moment-to-moment experiencing – or 'flow'. If we can make an effort to stay in our *experiencing* self, we can evade the clutches of our *narrative* self which keeps us stuck ruminating in all we are not, all we haven't done, all we should have done…

Here are a few quotes worth considering:-

---

**"Health is the greatest gift, contentment the greatest wealth."**

— THE BUDDHA

---

**"Pause in your chase of happiness, just pause, and be happy."**

— GUILLAUME APOLLINAIRE,
FRENCH POET

**"Realise that true happiness lies within you, you can't buy it.'"**

— OG MANDINO, AMERICAN AUTHOR

**"People are not disturbed by things, but by the view they take of them....Wealth consists not in having great possessions, but in having few wants."**

— EPICTETUS, STOIC PHILOSOPHER

**"Grant me the serenity to accept the things I can't change, the courage to change the things I can, and the wisdom to know the difference."**

— THE SERENITY PRAYER (WRITTEN
DURING THE GREAT DEPRESSION)

Now ask yourself the following questions:

- How contented/discontented do I feel right now on a scale of 1 to 5?
- Am I discontented about the past? If so, what about?
- Am I angry or discontented because I envy another for something they have? If so, who and what?
- Make a list of all the good things in your life. Include things like clean water and electricity, sewage pipes, free education, access to medical facilities and expertise, libraries, museums, local transport, friends, family and/or professionals who support you.
- Have you thought about what it would be like to live in poor parts of Africa, India or South America or somewhere war-torn? Read some accounts of life lived by people in need of The International Red Cross.

Now you have thought about the above questions, are you still as discontented as you were? If it has made a difference to your score, try doing this every time you feel really cheesed off. The reason this works it that it changes the story you are telling yourself, so it changes your reality.

Reasonable ambition is built into humans by evolution. But regularly stoking discontent, envy and anger makes us ill. Spend 10 minutes a day cultivating contentment by writing out a list of the things you are grateful for. You will see a change in your mood within a week.

The 'past' is based partly on fact and partly on our interpretation of it. Remind yourself every day: "I can't change events but I can change my responses."

## CATCH NASTY THOUGHTS

Alcoholics Anonymous has a famous phrase: 'Compare and despair'. If we allow ourselves to feel lesser than Instagram influencers or Facebook fibbers, are we cultivating the best of ourselves?

Listening to unspoken thoughts, as though eavesdropping on someone else's conversation, can be rather revealing. Very often our critical inner voice fosters inwardness, distrust, self-criticism, self-denial, addictions and a retreat from goal-directed activities.

Is this what you are hearing from your inner voice? Would you say such things to a beloved friend? Is what you hear true or just an opinion (an 'ought' not an 'is')? Are you mistaking feelings for facts? See *Thinking (Part 1, Chapter 3)* for more on this.

If what we overhear from ourselves is downright mean, then we have a problem with our self-esteem and this will express itself in the way we treat our partner and our kids as well as how we allow our partner to treat us.

The important question is how to shift this. We got this way for good reasons. If our parents were critical and hostile; or worse, neglectful and/or abusive, we will have incorporated their voice into how we talk to ourselves (and others). See *Attachment Styles (Part 2, Chapter 14)* for more on this.

It might be a good move to seek out some therapy if the negative self-talk feels utterly overwhelming and you can't shut it out. See *Other Resources (Part 6, Chapter 39)* for ideas on how to find a therapist.

But even without therapy, there are many proven ways to reduce the impact of the critical inner voice:

Get good at **identify**ing the **negative self-talk**. It often comes in the form of imagining what others are thinking about you, eg. 'They are going to make a fool of you', 'You can't trust anyone' but it can also appear as social anxiety, eg. 'I bet A thought I was stupid when I said/did X, Y, Z'.

Write down the thoughts as they come by making notes in your phone/notebook. Put in the thought, the time of day and the trigger if you can spot it, or make time at the end of the day to journal about what you have learnt from eavesdropping on yourself in a nice book you buy specially, to symbolise how you are coming to value your own feelings and thoughts.

If you start noticing that your negative self-talk is worse after spending half an hour on social media (everyone else's lives seem so much nicer than yours...) think twice about how much time you spend on Insta or Facebook.

When you hear criticism by yourself or others, ask yourself, 'Is this valid?' If you aren't sure, ask a trusted friend if they think it is valid and if they agree it is, then be prepared to address their criticism by changing your behaviour.

Playing the victim is not a helpful solution because it puts the need to change on someone else and *you* remain stuck in the same, unhappy place. Feelings are never wrong – they are just feelings, but we *are* responsible for what we *do* with our feelings. So on this note, remember no-one else is ever to blame for the actions *you* take, however provoking you may *feel* they have been! See *Coercive Control (Part 4, Chapter 26)* for more on this.

If your trusted friend confirms that your negative self-talk isn't justified, try the following: hold the thought in your mind, then at the same time do something pleasurable like singing a nursery rhyme, or doing a little dance. This works a bit like EMDR (an NHS-approved method for resolving traumatic memories) by separating the thought from its physiological effects (ie. how it *feels* to have the thought).

Another strategy is to replace each negative thought with a happy one by looking at a photograph of someone you know who loves you. Say to yourself, 'This amazing person thinks I am great, who am I to disagree with them?'

This might take some repetition but if you try it whenever you catch yourself having a negative thought, you will start to kick the habit which keeps you stuck in poor self-esteem.

It sounds obvious, but who we are depends in large part on whom we spend time with. Poor self-esteem is often caused by the double whammy of critical self-talk *and* allowing others in our lives to treat us disrespectfully.

If that is your partner, see *Difficult Behaviours* and *Bad Reactions (Part 4, Chapters 22 & 24)* for help on this. Examples of how company can impact our self-esteem might include 'friends' who always manage to say something which leave us stewing, who pick silly fights and make dramas out of everything, or who make a habit of leaving us out and/or being late to meet us.

Worksheet 5 enables you to examine what company you keep and how those people affect you during an average month:

| Name of person | What % of the time do I feel with them | | |
|---|---|---|---|
| | Positive | Neutral | Negative |
| | | | |
| | | | |
| | | | |

Notice where the negative percentages stack up and ask yourself, 'Can I see this person less? Or if they really matter to me, can I talk to them about how they make me feel? See *Opening Up A Conversation (Part 3, Chapter 19)* for ideas on how to start a difficult conversation.

Another way to stop negative self-talk is to put your attention on another person. It really is true that service to others undercuts negative self-talk because you can point to it in your head and say *Huh, if I am such a s\*\*\*, why did that person smile at me so gratefully when I did X or Y?* So try and do a kind deed for someone else every day. Earn that smile! It will counter the negative thoughts you send yourself.

It is undeniable that **the future is unknown**. Gloomy or cheery forecasts abound and either may be true. Confident people usually have goals in life - both short and longer term goals. Write down yours, make them measurable, achievable and keep returning to them every month to chart your progress. By making this commitment and seeing your progress, you will have concrete things to counter the flow of negative self-talk.

Decide what you like doing and practice doing it (for fun). You'll get better at it. Do deep breathing every day and some form of mindfulness (meditation has proven mental health benefits).

Engaging the body is important, as exercise produces feel-good body chemicals and also produces new brain cells. It is also critical because your body never lies. Other people and social media apps can manipulate you into believing they are good for you, but if you get good at listening to your gut, you will soon learn the truth. See *Keeping Calm (Part 1, Chapter 6)* for ideas on how to do this.

It is helpful to remember just to feel grateful to ourselves for feeding ourselves, cleaning our home/clothes, changing our bedsheets, even for brushing our teeth and cutting our nails. It may sound absurd but these acts of self-care are evidence we are cared about – by ourselves! Loving ourselves with an Act of Service at least every other day are important ways of signalling to ourselves that we are 'worth it'. In this sense, 'faking it 'til we make it' really does have benefits. Simple things like calling a supportive friend for a chat, taking the time for a candlelit bath, listening to a song we love or appreciating nature's beauty can all do the trick.

## BOOST THAT GRATITUDE PRACTICE

Neuroscientist Andrew Huberman (see *Other Resources - Part 6*) has shown how it is possible for us to make powerful shifts using a new kind of gratitude practice, which shifts us from defensive patterns into more trusting, confiding ones by reshaping the context in which we experience ourselves. What's even better is that he found his method works even when you are not actively thinking about it, ie. it hums along in the background having an effect on you no matter what else you are doing/thinking!

Unlike traditional gratitude practices which ask you to simply to count your blessings, his method involves concentrating on feeling into the experience of being the person who is *receiving* gratitude. So, if you are someone who often writes letters of thanks to people who did nice things for you, or you send your partner/friends/family loving texts and expressions of thanks, then you are a *potent* force for shifting other people's brain states into good places. Well done you!

But while it is a good idea to keep letters/voicemails of thanks from loved ones, it is clearly impractical to hang around hoping people will send you heartfelt expressions of thanks on a daily basis! So Huberman recommends reading/watching stories of people who got help from others and then noting down the following:

- **What the struggle was**
- **What the help was**
- **How the story impacted on you emotionally**

Then for just one minute (or two or three) a day, use these notes to feel into the emotional state that watching/reading the story originally produced in you. Hazlitt (see *Other Resources - Part 6*) showed this daily practice reduced amygdala activity (the part of the brain where fear is generated) and led to a significant reduction of two inflammatory chemicals released by stressed-out brain cells.

A TAKEAWAY

Learn to eavesdrop on your thoughts and you can turn the inside of your head into a place you would be happy to leave a child you loved, ie. somewhere caring, helpful and encouraging.

## Chapter 6

# Keeping Calm

Why is keeping calm important? We all know people who are always flustered, flapping, late. But it's not good for their gut, their heart, or their blood pressure. Nor is it any good for their relationship.

For our relationships to flourish, we need time together; time for mutual appreciation, time for tender touch. This can't happen if we don't know how to find a calm state of mind before we start out.

Biographies on successful people reveal how they were able to see the bigger picture, to set aside minor bumps in the road and to stick to a plan. One of the reasons they can do this is that they have worked to get their tempers under control!

- **Body and mind**
- **Angry in a fight**
- **Preparation for quality time**

## BODY AND MIND

If we are having difficulty identifying what we feel, we can listen to our body – our emotions stir first in our bodies, so if we listen carefully, we can discover what they are trying to tell us.

Perhaps it is helpful to understand that Western medicine and modern ideas about humanity, the human body and healing are both, well, modern and Western! Most people in the world, and across history, have seen and still do see, these things rather differently. In Bali, for example, falling asleep is seen as a sign of feeling scared, while in Vietnam, daily massage by family members is equivalent to saying 'How are you?' Different, huh?

"The West knows Best" agenda has undoubtedly conquered cholera, smallpox and Western medicine makes a good go at challenging the ravages of cancer. But our medical services are increasingly overwhelmed with patients suffering ailments caused by poor diet and bad mental health; eg. obesity, diabetes, depression, anxiety and so on. This is almost certainly because we don't listen to our body enough or put into practice the lessons we already know (eat 5 fruit/vegetables a day, do 10,000 steps).

Relationships often go wrong because one way we can get rid of emotions we don't like is to use someone else as our **psychic dustbin**. We all know the urban myth about the father who gets told off by his boss, goes home and shouts at his partner, who shouts at the kid who kicks the cat! Handing on unwanted emotions comes easily, but it doesn't serve us in the long run. Indeed, projected emotions simply come back to hit us round the head like boomerangs.

This is why learning to *identify* what you feel and *communicating* it *clearly* is so crucial to being able to live in loving relationships rather than fractious ones. Learning how to return to a calm state is a key step to achieving this.

Brain science tells us that emotions begin in the body. This makes sense of why ancient ways of caring for body *and* mind are increasingly popular in the West. These include yoga, tai chi and mindfulness and/or meditation. See *Other Resources - Part 6* for more on this.

## ANGRY IN A FIGHT

Rage evolved for good reasons. We need it to stand our ground, protect our young and conserve our resources. What I think is less well appreciated is that **rage** is usually masking a powerful **fear** response.

When rage circuits activate our older emotion systems in our mammalian brain, our prefrontal lobes (the part above the eyebrows responsible for rational thinking and empathy) shut down. This is why we can often say or do things we later regret when we are gripped in the vice of anger.

It is virtually impossible to stay truly enraged if the object of your fury is out of sight. So if you have a habit of seeing red and want to stop its negative effects, inform your partner *in a calm moment when you are not fighting* that you are going to try something different if and when things get heated between you. Tell them you are going to *leave* the room and only come back when you have calmed down. Explain to them it is essential they *don't* follow you as that will stop you calming down. Tell them you *will* come back and are *not* abandoning them and that you *will* return to discuss the issue.

Once you have walked away and put yourself somewhere quiet, practice this breathing exercise to bring yourself back to a calm state of mind. Put one hand over your heart and another over your belly. Breathe in through your nose to a count of 3, hold for 3 and exhale for 6. Repeat 10 times. The pressure against your heart and your belly simulates the experience of being safely held in a parent's arms when you were a baby. The longer out-breath to in-breath ratio stimulates your parasympathetic nervous system, responsible for 'tend, befriend' and 'rest, digest' behaviours. Stick at it and it *will* calm you down. As you breathe, think of someone you feel safe with and imagine holding their hand.

Another really helpful exercise is Dr. Daniel Siegel's SIFT-ing where you tune into the Sensations, Images, Feelings, and Thoughts that you're experiencing. This brings you into the moment to help you make a reasonable choice about what to do/say next. See *Feelings (Part 1, Chapter 2)* for more on this.

## PREPARATION FOR QUALITY TIME

So! We have decided to put in some quality time with our partner. Perhaps we have decided on what the activity is and have it planned. But it is worth using a ten-minute ritual to transition from the humdrum of everyday life into our special time together.

Any one of the following activities will prime our brains well:

- Put yourself in nature. Slow your walk right down until you can feel how you actually fall forward when you transfer your weight from one foot to the other. Then take each sense in turn to become acutely aware of what you can hear, see and smell.

10 minutes is long enough for this but obviously do longer if you like.

- Imagine programming yourself as a robot to rise, to turn, to take a step. This helps you become aware and grateful for your amazing body.
- Look at some happy photos or videos of when you were having a good time together. Deliberately recall happy moments to the point that they make you both smile and hopefully laugh.

These activities set up the optimum 'framing' for our enjoyment of quality time with our loved one. For more on the importance of framing, see *Asking the right questions (Part 3, Chapter 15)*.

# CHAPTER 7

## YOUR ANGER

- **What to do about it**

Anger is everywhere.

But it is useful to ask ourselves what anger-making things can we simply avoid? Why obsessively watch/read the News if it upsets us? There are so many dreadful things in the world that we cannot change and dwelling on them will raise our blood pressure and release stress chemicals which compromise our immunity and make us feel miserable. So let's make an effort to concentrate on the things we can change and/or influence.

If we are often afflicted by feeling angry, it is essential to start by believing that calming our anger is possible and indeed, that this is a preferable way to live. Anger is an emotion which causes bodily changes such as increased heart rate, frowning, tummy flutters and baring of teeth, for example.

Anger can bubble up without our conscious control but it always has triggers. These can be conscious or unconscious, but anger is almost always caused by fear or frustration; usually a combination of the two.

**Keeping calm is possible**, even under pressure, especially in fearful situations. Think about fire-fighters or lifeboat crew who face real personal danger but manage to stay calm during their rescues. How do they do this? Through training! The exercises below are ways to *train* ourselves to shift our emotions from one track to another.

## WHAT TO DO ABOUT IT

- If the cause of your anger is right in front of you, take yourself out of the room/immediate vicinity as it is very hard to stay enraged if the cause of your fury is no longer 'in your face'.

- Deep breathe for five minutes (breathe in for a count of 3, hold for 3, exhale for a count of 6 with one hand over your heart, the other over your belly). Anger circuits cause you to release adrenaline which primes your sympathetic nervous system, responsible for 'fight/flight' behaviours. Deep breathing reverses this and stimulates your parasympathetic nervous system instead. This parallel nervous system is what underpins our tend/befriend and rest/digest behaviours so engaging it will dampen our angry feelings.

- Think of something in your personal life that made you smile (the last time you saw a toddler laugh, for example, or the broad smile on the face of someone you love). Bring it to mind as fully as you can and then turn up the corners of your lips and grin broadly for at least five seconds (even if you feel really silly!)

- Change your posture, so that you stop slumping and stand up straight.

Now that you have controlled your anger and got yourself to a happier place, ask yourself what was the underlying emotion that drove your anger. Was it fear? Was it frustration? Was it resentment?

If the anger was caused by your partner, is it possible to find a time to talk to them and explain how their behaviour made you feel?

Think about what *their* reasons might be for behaving in this way. See if you can include in the conversation *why* they might have done/said what they said, because by modelling an empathic position they will be more likely to take up an empathic position towards you.

Try to put the problem between you and them, but don't blame *them* for *your* feelings. Just share the feeling and see whether you can help them empathise with your position.

See *Finding The Middle Ground* and *The Art of Negotiation (Part 3, Chapters 16 & 17)* for more help on this.

If your anger is caused by how people are behaving in faraway places, ask yourself, is there something practical you can do? Volunteer your time, donate to charity, fundraise? If there is action to take, take it. If there isn't, stop baiting yourself by reading about things you don't have the power to resolve. See *Anger With The World (Part 5, Chapter 34)* for more on this.

Sometimes, we can really struggle to control our anger and it spills out of us, hurting others through our words or our actions. We might feel terribly sorry this has happened and swear to our partner it won't happen again. But it is probably a pattern you recognise by now.

I imagine it took a relationship with someone when you were a child to make you angry enough to be violent as a grown-up, so my hunch is that it will take a therapeutic relationship to make you better. There is lots of support out there. See the section on *Violence (Part 4, Chapter 27)* for more on this.

# PART TWO

## FIRMING UP THE FOUNDATIONS

# CHAPTER 8

## EXPRESSING LOVE

Dr Gary Chapman wrote a best selling book on the five Languages of Love. They are:

- **Touch**
- **Words**
- **Gifts**
- **Acts of service**
- **Quality time**

Most of us have two love languages we speak in more often than the others. This is usually determined by what we observed our own caregivers doing when we were young. To find out what your main love languages are, have a go answering the following questions:

- Which of the 'languages' listed above do you normally speak in the course of a week?
- What about your partner?
- What languages of love did your parents speak? Is it the same as yours? What did your partner's parents speak? Is it the same as theirs?
- Are you and your partner speaking the same languages?

## TOUCH

How many ways could you touch your partner?

How many ways, in the average day, do you?

Where you do you like to be touched? Have you told your partner?

Have you asked your partner where they like to be touched?

## WORDS

Why do you like your partner? What about them did you appreciate today?

Have you the words to say so? If not, try writing them down. See *Expectations (Part 1, Chapter 4)* for ideas on this.

Have you asked your partner what words of love they want to hear?

Have you told them about the ways you love them?

## GIFTS

Not just the big birthday gift once a year, but everyday things like finding a stone on a beach, or a flower on a walk can help your partner know you are thinking about them when they are not there.

Could you return home with a bunch of flowers? What about some bubble bath and suggest you share a bath together?

Can you read aloud, or write out for them, a poem that you like?

Could you wrap a single chocolate?

Remember, it's the giving, not the gift, that matters. It really is true that it is the thought that counts because when we feel alive in someone else's mind, we feel *connected* and that is the ultimate goal of all relationship-building.

## ACTS OF SERVICE

Let's say you go out for a walk. An act of service could be as simple as opening a gate for them, or letting them go through a door first. Saying, "Let me do that for you" shows you care.

Do they like a cup of tea in the morning? Could you bother to make them one?

Are they particular about having a clean floor? In which case, could you get out the mop more often than under a blue moon?!

What about doing any other form of routine domestic heroism that they say they mind about? For example, if they always complain that they are the one who cleans the kitchen, could you do that for them one night after supper, to show you are holding them in mind?

Have you asked them what big or little jobs they might appreciate you doing for them this week? Having asked them, did you actually do them?

When you have performed an Act of Service, can you check that they liked it: "Did I do that right? Is that how you like it?"

## QUALITY TIME

Anything can be turned into quality time if we try to make it fun and a shared activity. It doesn't have to be something flashy to qualify. See *Quality Time (Part 2, Chapter 11)* for more on this.

## A TAKEAWAY

Not all the love languages will suit you/your partner, but the key thing is to identify which ones *they* speak and talk to them in it. Then get them to read this chapter so they can do the same for you.

## Chapter 9

# Ancient Words for Love

The English language has only one word for describing love which is, well, love! But the Ancient Greeks had seven. They are as applicable today as they were 2,500 years ago. If you are trying to evaluate why your relationship is creaking, or how it has ended up on the ropes, then examining the different ways you love (or don't love) your partner will be useful.

- **Types of love**
- **Put them into practice**

## Types of Love

- ***Ludus*** - *playful*
- ***Eros*** - *sexual*
- ***Pragma*** - *compassionate*
- ***Philia*** - *friendship*
- ***Philautia*** – *self-love*
- ***Storge*** – *familial*

- **_Agape_** - *humanitarian*

**Ludus** (pronounced 'loo-duss') refers to a playful sort of love. Flirting, banter, playing practical jokes, rough-and-tumble play, joshing – all these would be English equivalents to *ludus*. It may lead to becoming lovers but doesn't necessarily have to. In fact, it is commonly how we 'love' children by doing rough-and-tumble games with them and/or playing actual games (cards, boardgames etc.)

Does your partner enjoy practical jokes? If you aren't sure, ask yourself if they like playing them on you. If the answer is yes, they probably do! Can you invest in some props for this? Rubber eggs that bounce, plastic ice cubes with spiders inside them and even a good old whoopee cushion will bring a smile to their face! Surprises are fun! What's more, the joy of anticipation once you have set up the joke is exciting for you too.

**Eros** will be familiar to anyone who has 'fallen in love' and had it requited. It is the feeling of going weak at the knees when you think of them, especially when the thoughts are sexual! The English phrase 'madly in love' comes closest to what the Greeks meant by Eros. It is a roller-coaster experience and no mistake, but remember, Eros is like using cardboard to start a fire. It burns really bright but only for a short time. After that, it will be the logs of your shared values and interests and how you show kindness to one another that will keep the fire alive.

Sexual connection matters as what makes your partner different from your friends/other family relationships is that you have a sexual as well as an emotional bond with them. Eros burns brightest at the beginning of a relationship when the fire burns without effort, but that doesn't mean it can't be helped along with erotica, lingerie and role play later on. Marital sex might be 'mating in captivity' to quote Esther Perel, but it absolutely doesn't have to be boring!

For more on imaginative ways to connect to your partner, consult the brilliant, American couples therapist, Esther Perel. See *Other Resources (Part 6)*.

**Pragma** gives us the English word 'pragmatic' meaning a person is more concerned with matters of fact that what could or should be. Pragma is a longstanding, forgiving sort of love; what we might call cherishing. It is patient, unselfish and underpins contented, happy partnerships. The Biblical verse often trotted out at weddings from Corinthians 1 (13:4-8) describes it well: *Love is patient, love is kind* etc.

To check your pragma is alive and well, ask yourself what Acts of Service you have done for your partner this week? (See the previous chapter on *Expressing Love (Part 2, Chapter 8)* for more on this.)

**Philia** means fondness, amity and affinity and is the kind of love which underpins deep, enduring friendships. It is long-term, supportive and benign, an accepting and approving kind of love you feel towards the person.

You wouldn't dream of going out with a friend and not asking them how they are, but it is all too easy to forget to treat our partner and/or children with the same basic care.

Remember they need philia too, so try to check in every day.

'How are you?' can be ducked easily, especially if you are asking them while actually doing something else. If we don't give the other person our full attention while asking this question, we are unconsciously communicating that we don't *really* want to know the answer and this behaviour, repeated over time, may make them feel neglected and sad.

Asking, *'What made you smile today?'*, *'What made you sad?'* or *'What made you cross?'* are good ways to draw our loved one out of their shell because it requires them to tell a story, rather than just grunt, *'Fine'*. These questions are useful ways to get kids talking about what happened in their day.

**Philautia** combines *philia* with the Greek word *auto* meaning self, so it is the benign end of narcissism where we believe we are deserving of being well-treated by others. It underpins self-confidence and the belief that another can love you properly. It is absolutely not the malign end of self-love where too much 'me, me, me' damages our 'we' relationships.

To check your *philautia* is up to scratch, have a read of *Improving Self-Esteem (Part 1, Chapter 5)* for more on this aspect of love.

**Storge** (pronounced 'store-gay') is the love which powers all family relationships. It is the love which makes a parent care about their child, a brother about their sister, a child for a grandparent. But it can cause conflicts of interest for the couple – there is a reason mother-in-law jokes proliferate in every culture! It is not so easy to stomach that old injunction, 'Love me, love my family!'

When you met, your partner had a web of pre-existing relationships which supported them. It isn't loving of you to resent them for wanting to maintain these relationships now. If you/your partner argue about wider family relationships and it feels like conflicts of interest often arise, it might be important to examine this further. See *Difficult Behaviours (Part 4, Chapter 24)*.

**Agape** means brotherly love or charity. It underpins humanitarian feelings and is essential for societies to function effectively, but not that relevant to personal relationships. It is the feeling which disposes you to donate to Comic Relief or Children in Need, for example.

## PUTTING THEM INTO PRACTICE

Try these on your own, or better still, with your partner/child:

- Write down the seven Greek words for love, rating how important they are to *you* from most important to least important
- Next to each one, list the ways you demonstrated that particular kind of love to your loved one in the last week/last two weeks/month.
- If you have done the exercise together, now compare your lists. Do they match up in terms of which type of love is most important and which is least important? If they don't, what jumps out about the way you have weighted your choices?
- Can you share ways you would like to have the seven kinds of love demonstrated to you each week/month?
- Can you make an agreement to attempt this and check back in to see how you did at a specified future date?

# CHAPTER 10

## LAUGHTER

On a sundial I once saw, it said, 'The day is wasted that we have not laughed'.

You will know that kindness almost always produces a smile.

So how can you bring more laughter, smiling and humour into your relationship?

This is so important I think we should delve into the science behind it. At a brain chemical level, laughing reduces adrenaline and cortisol (both stress hormones) and releases your own homemade opiates (endorphins). It even enhances the efficiency of your T-cells, which improves your immune system.

The physical act of laughing works out important muscles around your eyes and mouth which are linked through the vagus nerve to your stomach, heart and lungs. A highly responsive vagus nerve (known as 'high vagal tone') is extremely good news for your health, as the vagus nerve is the immune system's communication super highway bringing information about the state of the body to the mind.

Laughing increases your vagal tone; what is more, it is impossible to feel anger, guilt or resentment while you are laughing. Humour and smiling may not have quite the same physical benefits as laughing, but their overall effects are beneficial too.

## EXERCISES TO GIGGLE MORE

There are passive things you can do together like looking at funny photos online or watching comedy. But even more beneficial are active ways of having fun. Why not try to:

- learn the steps of a new dance together
- dance together to a favourite song
- write a story one sentence at a time, alternating you then them
- write a poem about something you saw together then read it aloud
- read a poem you love aloud to them and ask them to read one to you
- sing them a soppy song (Youtube has plenty of singalong options) then get them to sing you one
- do a word puzzle together
- sit down side-by-side and work on a creative activity, eg. drawing/painting/crafts of some description

Try to ensure the activity involves three key things: **touch**, **eye contact** and **laughter**.

## Chapter 11

## Quality Time

It is amazing how much difference spending an hour or two of quality time with your partner can make to the atmosphere between you. Many contented couples have 'date nights' and for good reason because leaving the familiar and going somewhere novel gets your brain's dopamine and endorphins going (the brain's feel-good chemicals).

John Gottman's research has shown that a happy partnership has five nice interactions for every fractious one. This is a useful rule of thumb to remember when you are reflecting on how your relationship is going. So why not try to make a point of saying nice things to your partner as often as you can?

- **Money is tight**
- **It's raining**

## MONEY IS TIGHT

So, you have decided to have a date night, perhaps it is even Valentine's Day. But what if money is tight? Going out for dinner is expensive; ruinously so, especially if you have small children at home and must pay a babysitter…

Let's suppose you have enjoyed either a holiday to Greece or a TV programme about it in the past and thought a particular dish looked good. Decide on a night you are both free, look up a recipe and shop for the ingredients together. Cook it together side-by-side then eat the fruits of your labour, perhaps even share the plate. If you have any, look at the photos and videos you have from a trip preferably on a bigger screen than your phone. Then after dinner, look up 'Hasapiko' on YouTube and fall about laughing as you try to learn this Greek dance. Pause for plenty of smiles and hugs.

If you manage this in good cheer, you will have found several ways to generate the flow of feel-good endorphins and the bonding neurotransmitter, oxytocin. Sharing food, exercise, and laughing are three important activities which get these flowing. Nor will you have had to spend lots of money, had to encounter other couples to whom you might compare yourselves, or eat underwhelming food!

## IT'S RAINING

Let's suppose it's too wet to go out. Yes, of course, you can sit around and moan about it… but you could also look up *Singing in the Rain*, the old song and dance routine and do it together. Do it badly, try again and do it a little better! It's FUN!

My point is that quality time doesn't have to cost a lot of money or depend on a sunny day. If you are dismissing this, is it because you consider yourself too old, too serious, too pompous, too worried, too lazy or too busy?

Let me bring you back to the science again. Cardio experts predict than an hour spent as above will add an hour to your life expectancy. Who is the silly one now?!

For more on the science of laughter, see *Other Resources (Part 6)*.

# Chapter 12

## Communicating Well

Why does communication matter?

Well, talking to each other is how we tell our partner/child what is going on inside us. They *can't* read *our* mind and *we* can't read *theirs*, however sure we might feel about what they are thinking. We have to remember that what we feel about ourselves is the glasses we are wearing all the time when we imagine how they see us. This is why if we feel good about ourselves, we will be likely to think we are loved and vice versa.

If we don't understand why someone behaves the way they do, we can't empathise with them. If we can't empathise with our partner/child, we will be tempted to behave contemptuously towards them. Speaking in a contemptuous tone is one of the biggest predictors of relationship failure down the line, as Dr. Gottman has discovered.

- **Noticing your habits**
- **Changing the game**
- **Developing romantic competency**

## Noticing your Habits

To save energy the human brain creates shortcuts - we call them habits. Our ways of speaking to our partner/child are habits, often unhelpful ones, especially when residual resentment creeps into every nook and cranny of our discourse.

If our tone is angry, it will unconsciously trigger the release of cortisol, the stress hormone, in *their* brain. Once that happens, they will stop listening and return our anger, via *their* tone of voice and facial expressions.

But if we can keep calm and use humour where possible, we can talk so they *will* listen.

Changing patterns is hard. It takes practice and application - but it can be done.

We will need to try, try and try again before they hear our message, especially when the information is new. Be patient and give them plenty of time to take in what you are saying.


## Developing Romantic Competency

Joanne Davila is an American academic psychologist whose TED talk, Skills for Healthy Romantic Relationships, is well worth a watch (see the entry on Emotion in Other Resources in Part 6). After much research, she identifies three key skills which enable us to make and maintain healthy relationships. These are:

- **1. Insight**
- **2. Mutuality**
- **3. Emotion regulation**

***Insight*** means using what you already know about *your partner* to identify when their annoying behaviour relates to a problem in the relationship and when it is simply reflective of what they are like.

---

> eg. Your partner is late to a date. If you know they are always late to everything, you can shrug it off. Or you can feel affronted, resentful, and the nice date is ruined if you don't use your insight.

---

It also means using what you know about *yourself*.

---

> eg. Early on in your relationship, your partner mentions they would like an open relationship. You go away and do some journalling on this topic, analysing carefully what you think and feel. Having done so, you come back to them saying, 'You know, for me, that wouldn't work and if it is a deal-breaker for you, then the relationship must end'. Sad, but at least you stopped it before you fell for them and ended up broken-hearted.

---

***Mutuality*** means recognising two key things: first, you *both* have needs and secondly, these needs may not sync up perfectly. If you fully accept this truth, then you can express what you would like calmly and openly, encouraging them to do the same, then negotiate your way to a good place.

eg. You get offered a great job but realise it will mean you have to travel more. You say to your partner, 'It really matters to me that I get to take this job but I realise it may impact on our time together. If I give up doing X to spend more time with you, do you think we could make it work?'

**Emotion Regulation** is the third critical skill to develop because over-reacting with anger or withdrawal-type behaviours alienates your partner and stops them empathising with your distress. Learning to tolerate uncomfortable emotions, not act on them impulsively, enables you to think through your decisions calmly.

eg. You are anxious because your partner has gone out with friends but hasn't texted you to say goodnight. Your jealousy fantasies are running out of control and you are checking your phone every two seconds. Emotion regulation means saying kindly to yourself, 'Don't worry, they will text when they are ready, they do love you and you are safe in this relationship. Now you are going to put your phone away and go and have a hot bath.'

## Changing the Game

The above section is the big picture focus, but let's zoom in on the micro aspect of communication. Did you know, only about 50% of the message you are conveying is done by the words you choose? The rest of it comes through three other modes, all of them non-verbal:

- tone of voice
- facial expression
- body language

Non-verbal communication is habitual, meaning it is controlled by your unconscious mind. This means it depends on your mood, where a mood is an unconscious background state you may not be aware of.

Learning to match your non-verbal communication to the words you are using is a skill you can learn. There is often a disconnect between what we see in another's face, how our body and emotions react to their face, and how blind our conscious mind is to this complex and nuanced process.

The exercises below are *essential* because they will teach you how to make your non-verbal and verbal messages *congruent* (ie. matching). This is useful in all dealings with anyone, anywhere. It's worth persisting in to perfect.

---

**Exercise 1**: Open your phone camera and film yourself saying, *'Darling of course I love you'*

---

Try saying it once, without much thought, as you usually might, then play it back. Then try saying it robotically, no emphasis anywhere. Then say it impatiently and dismissively, then compassionately and lovingly.

Have a go at listing a few common phrases you use to communicate every day with your partner. Things like:

'Who's walking the dog? What do you want for supper? Have you made the kids' packed lunches?'

Now have a go saying each common phrase with one of the following three emotions in your heart:

- irritation
- contempt
- resentment

[To conjure up the right emotional state, shut your eyes and spend 15 seconds summoning up the last time you felt that emotion intensely, then open your eyes and say into the camera the commonplace phrase.]

Play the videos back and watch how each emotion playing across your face and seeping out from your tone distorts your communication. Powerful, huh?

---

**Exercise 2:** Record each phrase below using your video app then watch yourself back. Concentrate on what your eyes do and how each version makes you feel.

---

1. Say *That's great!* With enthusiasm, as good news.

Now say it in a downbeat, dismissive way.

2. Say *I'm sorry* or *Sorry.* Make it an apology full of genuine regret. Make eye contact by staring at the camera's dot and really emphasise the first syllable ['so'] of sorry.

Now say it in a defensive way. Notice the emphasis passes to 'I'm' and how your eyes slide away and you frown.

3. Say *Yes* genuinely. Eyes open, said quickly with a slight nod of your head.

Now say it slowly, reluctantly. Eyes sliding away, lips a bit sneery.

4. Say *Tomorrow?* as a genuine, open question.

Now say it as if the suggestion is absurd, notice how your nose wrinkles into a sneer and your eyes look away.

5. Say *Thanks a lot!* Genuinely with your eyes open. Now say it with the emphasis on 'lot'. Notice how you frown and your head drops.

6. Say *What's up?* Eager and sharing with genuine concern. Now say it dismissively, impatiently. Notice how the deadpan your delivery is in this mood.

7. Say *I've been busy*! As a statement of fact said with pride. The emphasis on "I've" implies others haven't been busy, while the emphasis on "busy" implies defensiveness.

8. Say *It's getting late!* As a statement of shared fact. Now say it as an implication of impatience and see if you can notice how putting the emphasis on "late" implies blame.

Hopefully, having done these exercises, you can observe how powerful tone of voice and facial expression are in conveying a message. In essence, they produce the **mood** of your communication.

Can you reflect on how your habitual ways of communicating with your partner or child may actually interfere with their ability to receive your **message** clearly?

## A TAKEAWAY

Calm and kindness are the keys to good communication. The more you talk about what you feel and why, the more you enable your partner/child to empathise with you and the closer you will feel to each other.

See *Keeping Calm (Part 1, Chapter 6)* and *Learning to Listen (Part 2, Chapter 13)* for more on this.

## CHAPTER 13

# LEARNING TO LISTEN

In most walks of life, we soon learn that practice makes perfect. Communication – which in essence means getting your message across - benefits from both preparation and practice.

The assumption here is that you are the one suggesting change, but have been met by incomprehension or objections from your partner/child.

For some people, both brevity and listening are unnatural. If you often end up fighting rather than talking, have a read of *Keeping Calm (Part 1, Chapter 6)* first.

## Do's

Look at your partner/child in an interested, concerned, loving way. Nod in understanding. Don't tap your fingers, sigh with impatience, frown or sneer.

Seek clarification after they speak but *don't* immediately challenge or deny their view.

[Use their name, then say] *Can you clarify that a bit for me?* [Let them talk on]

[Then say] *OK if I've got that right, what you are saying is 'xxxx'* [repeat what they said, then ask] *Is that right?*

If the issue or objections are still unclear, or impossible, respond with:

*Yes I can see that, but have you thought about…* [introduce complication 1. If they accept this, pause, then introduce complication 2].

Without anger or impatience it is possible for both of you to see both points of view. Using the phrase, '*What can* **we** *do about it?*' frames the issue as a shared problem, not a clash of wills.

You will often be met by blame or accusations from your partner/child. Don't deny or counter blame. Try saying instead:

*Yes there may be some truth in that, but the issue now is what are we going to change from now on?*

Pause, stay silent and defuse their anger partly through saying the above and partly through body language, ie. nodding, keeping eye contact, not folding your arms or crossing legs.

---

[Continue with:] *Remember I started the chat because I'm concerned about X...*

---

Very useful phrases, ideally accompanied by touch, are to use their name, followed by:

- *We don't seem to be getting very far today* [or if anger is arising]
- *I can see we are both getting tired* [don't say 'angry', then:]
- *Let's think a bit and talk again on xxx day* [agree a date].

End with an upbeat smile and touch. Show optimism, not defeated resentment.

## DON'TS

Using the phrases 'You *always*' and 'You *never*' will predictably be denied or excused with counter blame.

*Why?* and *I know that!* said abruptly, are challenges not only to the facts, but also to your partner/child as a communicating Other. Try to avoid them as they will only provoke defensiveness and anger.

If they make an unexpected, difficult announcement or suggestion, it is better to respond, *Interesting, how would that work?* to get them talking. It gives you time to think, respond casually and slowly; not fearfully or angrily.

*Yeah, have we thought about…* by inserting a *'we'* you prevent an immediate clash of wills. Using the word *'we'* gives you time to raise practical questions (not objections) to their plan and to prime your own brain to think about the 'we' of your partnership/parent relationship, rather than slide into self-orientated, 'me me me' concerns.

Practice by examining all your common usages. Rule out impatience or blame. Start with a bonding phrase such as their name or an endearment. Use touch as a bond where appropriate.

Remember, *tone of voice* and *body language* set the mood of the conversation. Keep those respectful and the chat will go better.

See *Communicating Well (Part 2, Chapter 12)* for more on this.


## A TAKEAWAY

If you want to persuade someone of something you will have more success if you:

1. *Prepare* what you want to say
2. Say it as *briefly* as possible, then
3. *Listen* to what they have to say, respectfully!

# CHAPTER 14

## ATTACHMENT STYLES

It may unfortunately be true that right now, you or your partner simply don't have a strong enough self-image, therefore can't trust/share/give or accept love wholeheartedly.

Let's look at some difficult-to-feel feelings:- *sad, lonely, bored, hurt, not understood, confused, anxious, angry, untrusting.*

Are these a feature of your relationship?

If so, ask yourself the following questions and then write down the answers:

- Did you bring these feelings with you into this relationship?
- Have these kinds of feelings bothered you at other
- times in your life? eg. When relating to your own parents as a child, or in previous sexual relationships?

- Can you imagine either of your parents felt these difficult feelings in their own partnership? In what ways might their relationship resemble your own?
- What did your parents repeatedly tell you about *you*?
- What do you know about how your partner's parents spoke to them about *them*?

* * *

- **Types of attachment**
- **You are not alone**
- **What to do about it**
- **Steps for Change**

How we love as grown-ups depends on how we were loved as infants and the brain circuits governing this behaviour are stored in unconscious parts of our minds over which we do not have conscious control. You got this way before you can remember, during the period of brain development between 0 and 3 years of age, so your attachment style (which is just a scientific way of saying 'how you love and expect to be loved') is essentially baked in – we could call it the emotional equivalent to breathing!

Our attachment style as grown-ups is largely hidden from view except when we are in stressful situations. If separation is looming, conflict is occurring or we feel at risk of abandonment, our attachment patterns will be triggered.

## TYPES OF ATTACHMENT

You were born incredibly dependent and unbelievably needy. Let's just remember that for the first five months of your life, you couldn't even roll over from your back to your tummy!

To thrive (not just survive) you needed a *reliable* caregiver to give you unconditional love and attention. See *Emotions* and *Feelings (Part 1, Chapters 1 & 2)* for more on this.

If this was not forthcoming, either because our caregiver was mentally ill or caught up in traumatic happenings, we learnt *not to expect* the other to meet our needs. This was adaptive at the time, as it was less painful than being continually let down.

Our young brain developed fast because it had to. We learnt from what we experienced, filing it away for future use. Habits, assumptions, ways of playing it safe emotionally-speaking, were all baked in to our brain circuitry by 3 years of age and are stored unconsciously as predictions about how others will behave towards us when we are upset.

If you or your partner seem to blow hot and cold, are overly clingy and/or avoidant of emotional closeness, then you/they may be *insecurely attached*. About 40% of the population fall into this category. There are four types of attachment category. They are:

**Secure** (60% of the population) You are able to see your lover's/child's point of view because you make space to listen to them; when they communicate clearly you can empathise with their position; you find close relationships relatively easy to sustain.

**Insecure Avoidant** (16%) When your lover/child approaches, you back off. eg. after being intimate, you need to distance yourself in a way which feels subtly (or blatantly) hurtful to them. You find yourself withdrawing when things get tricky and can struggle to express yourself. Partners/children might sometimes accuse you of 'stone-walling' and get frustrated/upset by your emotional distance.

**Insecure Ambivalent** (16%) You blow hot and cold. eg. one minute you want closeness, the next you seem not to care. We could say you crave the love but distrust the lover. You might be prone to irrational jealousy and/or find yourself feeling very insecure about your body/looks. You may need a lot of reassurance and feel very hurt when you don't get it.

**Insecure Disorganised** (6%) You behave in highly inconsistent ways, you can be unreliable, prone to promiscuity and/or very controlling of your partner/child. Your relationship problems stem from an abusive/traumatic childhood in which you felt very unsafe and/or were neglected yourself. The journey to health is long – you can get there – but you will probably need Professional Help. See *Other Resources - Part 6.*

## YOU ARE NOT ALONE

My guess is that if you and your partner are securely attached, you probably won't be reading this book, as your relationship is fine. So if you identify with any of the three insecure attachment styles described here, or recognise them in your partner, the first thing to realise is that you make up over one-third of the general population, so you are not alone.

The key thing to consider is this: the *upset child inside* you or your partner has not gone anywhere. It lives inside you/your partner and behaves just as you would expect a child in that position to behave, but *only* when it feels rejected or abandoned.

Think of the problem like this: imagine you are a transatlantic pilot flying a Boeing 767 from London to New

York with 375 passengers on board. But whenever you get het up (eg. your partner disagrees with you and an argument starts), your upset child inside takes control of the cockpit and the result is, well, disastrous. The plane nosedives and the disaster scenario follows a well-worn, all-too-familiar plot line for you both, always ending up in both partners feeling some toxic cocktail of despair, loneliness and anger.

The way to stop this is, in one sense, incredibly simple: you realise when your child is in the cockpit, you ask your adult self look after your upset child self and then your adult self can take back the controls. But to do this in practice is very hard because a child doesn't necessarily recognise their own behaviour is unreasonable (if you have wrangled with any toddlers recently, you will know what I mean!)

So it may take many flights before you are able to spot when the child is even *in* the cockpit and many goes after that before you start to believe your adult self is *capable* of looking after your distressed and traumatised child (after all, your caregiver(s) couldn't, or you wouldn't be in this mess in the first place). Only at this point, can you start to make different decisions and get that plane to New York on time. The old adage applies: 'If you always do what you always did, you'll always get what you always got'.

If you want to know more about any of these attachment styles, look up my blog post about *attachment theory* called 'Pull Yourself Together: Or Why You Can't' at www.psychoanalysisinotherstories.com. Another interesting avenue to research is to look up the 'Adult Attachment Interview', a research method used to figure out you/your partner's attachment style.

## What to do about it

The good news is that the brain is 'neuroplastic' meaning we can change our wiring right up until we take our last breath.

If you and/or your partner want to become reliable, trustworthy lovers, then the Science shows you can change an insecure attachment pattern into a secure one.

The key to this shift is getting good at knowing what you feel (spotting your inner child's characteristic ways of responding when things get stormy), communicating what you are feeling calmly to your partner (rather than sending the Boeing 747 into a nose-diving tail spin) and being patient about you/your partner's mistakes along the way.

## Steps for Change

The following questions for you to answer at your leisure in your Journal will encourage self-reflection and help you craft a coherent narrative. Spending time with these questions is doing something incredibly important because it will be changing your brain! I thank Dr. Lisa Firestone and Dr. Daniel Siegel for their contribution to the following Steps for Change section. To do this work with more of their helpful input, see their e-course offering: https://ecourse.psychalive.org

### Step 1: Family Background

Who was in your family? Include significant adults, siblings, etc. What was it like growing up in your family? How would you sum up your parents' philosophy about raising children?

## Step 2: Family Relationships and Attachment

Was there anyone in your life, other than your parents, who served as a parental figure or to whom you felt attached? Please state a few words to reflect your relationship with those individuals as well.

What were the major conflicts in your family?

Did you have conflict with anyone?

Was there anyone you could turn to, or any place you could go to, to help you feel comforted during difficult times?

## Step 3: Childhood Experiences

Did you ever experience a long separation from your parents in childhood? What was that like for you?

How were you disciplined as a child?

Have you ever felt threatened by your parents?

Have you ever felt rejected by your parents?

## Step 4: Looking Back On Your Early Relationships

Choose five adjectives or words that reflect your relationship with your mother or mother-like figure. Try to think back as far as you can remember to your early childhood.

Now, try to think of a memory or an incident that would illustrate each of the words you chose to describe the relationship. Write these memories or incidents down.

Repeat this exercise to describe your relationship with your father or father-like figure.

Adjective 1:
Memory:

Adjective 2:
Memory:

Adjective 3:
Memory:

Adjective 4:
Memory:

## Step 5: Identifying your Traumas

List some emotional or physical traumas or traumatic events that have happened in your life. These do not have to be "Big T" traumas. A trauma can be any significant, distressing event or incident that shaped you as a child – things that made you feel bad, scared, ashamed, etc.

1.
2.
3.
4.
5.
6.
7.
8.
9.
10.

## Step 6: Crafting Your Narrative

Now you have taken the time and effort to reflect on these questions, it is time to craft a coherent narrative from your reflections. The following tips will help you create a coherent, emotionally-engaged and powerful story to make sense of your childhood experiences.

- Write as an adult
- Write rationally
- Write autobiographically
- Write intuitively
- Write with feeling
- Write about how your past influences the present
- Write with balance
- Write with self-compassion

Try to do this in a Curious Open Accepting Loving (C.O.A.L.) manner and keep going until you have incorporated all the reflections you made in Steps 1 to 5. When you have completed it, let your partner and/or kids read it. It will help them be compassionate to you and when you find your critical inner voice is shouting, read your narrative again and use it to generate compassion for your past self who suffered so.

## A TAKEAWAY

Understanding how you were loved as a child is the key to changing how you love as an adult. This is deep stuff, mostly stored in our unconscious mind, so if you feel frustrated by your lack of progress, you might want to try some psychodynamic psychotherapy as it goes deep to reach this stuff. See the section on *Seeking Professional Help* in *Part 6*.

See *Emotions, Feelings, Expressing Love, Improving Self-Esteem* and *Expectations (Parts 1 & 2)* for more helpful reading in this area.

# PART THREE

## TIME TO CHANGE

## Chapter 15

# Asking the Right Questions

- **What is a good question?**
- **Framing**

## What is a good question?

The best sort of question is genuinely open-ended.

Said in a kind tone, "What would you like for supper?" could sound like a gift. "Pizza for supper?" is also a question, but could sound controlling, by inviting objections rather than seeking cooperation.

When it comes to deciding bigger issues, like a car or holiday for example, clearly inviting co-operation is better. Rather than saying, "I've chosen this hotel", you might say, "I have done some research and this seems to be a good option. What do you think?" Or, "This is going to be quite expensive to do. What are our priorities, do you think? Cost? Comfort? Convenience?"

When you limit your partner's choices and assume their answers, it can feel bullying to them. Salesmen are trained to ask, "Your pen or mine?" thereby reducing the customer's choice from whether or not they want the product to a choice of pen! That may work if you are trying to sell a car and will never see the customer again, but if you are in an ongoing relationship, you need *The Art of Negotiation (Part 3, Chapter 17)* not bully tactics.

In a long-term relationship, it is far better to turn the decision into a shared exploration, adventure, joint experience. And, as with all utterances, tone of voice really matters.

Ill-considered questions can invite resistance or resentment. For example, "What's the time?" said in a certain tone and in a particular context can be easily misconstrued as 'You are late!'

There is an art to steering a conversation. When they have spoken, you must **listen**. Then nod to show you have heard them. Then ask without challenge, *"How exactly would we do that?"* or, *"Have you thought about…?"* in a calm, kind tone. See *Learning to Listen* (Part 2, Chapter 13) for more on this.

## FRAMING

Psychology has shown that how a product is "framed" matters a lot. Essentially, association overrides content. For example, a yoghurt labelled '90% fat free' sells far more of the exact same yoghurt that when it is labelled '10% fat'.

Framing is something we pick up habitually, which means it operates unconsciously, outside our conscious awareness. Applying this to being in a relationship means that if you frame the question of where to go on holiday with shared, positive associations to previous happy holidays, your partner's brain is primed to respond to the topic in a helpful, friendly way.

For more on this, see *Thinking (Part 1, Chapter 3).*

## Chapter 16

## Finding the Middle Ground

- **Why negotiate?**
- **How to find the middle ground**

### Why Negotiate

You might think negotiation is something which only belongs in the workplace, but as any parent knows, good parenting involves endless horse-trading: *You can have your biscuit when I've put you in the buggy* or, *You can have your phone back when you've tidied your room*.

You will also know that once the first flush of love gives way to the two of you trying to find a way to thrive together, arguments are inevitable when pre-existing assumptions about a particular issue rise to the surface.

The *middle ground* is the place you need to find for your partnership to feel like a fair and kind place to be for both of you.

Negotiation is something we do with ourselves most minutes of every day. 'Shall I eat a biscuit or a carrot?' 'Should I have another cup of coffee?' 'Should I have pudding?' All these choices are negotiations between different parts of us, eg. our greedy self wants the biscuit, the healthy part knows we shouldn't!

When it comes to negotiating with our partner, it gets even more complicated, as we must negotiate with the different parts of ourselves *and* the different parts of them!

## How to Find the Middle Ground

Hopefully, you have already done some work thinking about what you *do and don't* value in your relationship and what you hope to change. If you haven't, please see *Feelings* and *Expectations* in *Part 1*.

Your wish to change assumes that both you <u>and</u> your partner need to do things differently in future. The question arises as to why your partner is not already doing what you would prefer? You need to give this some thought.

Finding the middle ground involves some preparation on your part. Follow these stepping stones to find it:

- Write down your top 3 or 4 most important relationship issues.
- Examine in detail your own assumptions. Find those flawed 'oughts' if you can. See *Thinking, (Part 1, Chapter 3)*.
- Ask or guess from the ideas above why your partner is not co-operating. Have circumstances changed? Are they under outside pressures from work or parents? Could selfishness, resentment, even malice

be behind it? Or are they just not noticing? In which case, have you explained how it makes you feel? Could it be their underlying beliefs about gender roles or their need to display their status to the world beyond? Are you/they falling into a gradual relapse of copying parents or other role models?

- Really try (and this *is* hard) to understand that your partner has, or believe they have, good reasons for doing what they do. After all, *you* do!

- Understand that you will probably be dealing with the thinking *behind* the behaviour which may be unconscious to both of you at this point.

- Try (and this is even harder!) to evaluate whether your partner might actually be right, half-right, or even partly justified to take up the position they have taken.

- Write down, from what your partner has said in previous arguments, why they might be doing what they are doing. What reasons might they propose for opposing the change you want?

- Figure out their (and your) emotions behind the behaviour you want to change. This is the smartest way forward.

- If their feelings, needs, emotions can be satisfied in another way, the change you are asking for is easier to manage.

- Get creative. This means challenging your own assumptions and habits since the chances are you have gone on about this change you would like to see previously, to no avail.

- Ask yourself what are you prepared to compromise on, i.e. where is *your* middle ground? Ask your partner to make a list of the issues which are bothering them about you. Then horse-trade until you find the middle ground!

Studies by Nobel Prize winner Daniel Kahneman (father of behavioural science) have shown us that humans feel small losses far more keenly than even quite big gains. I like the quote from his book, *Thinking, Fast and Slow*:

---

"Our comforting conviction that the world makes sense rests on a secure foundation: our almost unlimited ability to ignore our ignorance."

---

Kahneman has shown how losing a £5 bet is heavier in emotional terms than winning £5. So find things your partner would be sad to lose, if you want them to change their behaviour for you.

I suggest listing three or four issues, not just your top one. This is because it is easier to negotiate simpler issues then build on your relationship's confidence in tacking the bigger ones.

Remember, professional negotiators say 90% of negotiation takes place before the parties even meet. This means if you want to find the middle ground, you have to *plan* before you start the conversation. To learn how to do this, read the next chapter, *The Art of Negotiation (Part 3, Chapter 17),* which lays out the seven preparatory steps to achieving your desired outcome.

# CHAPTER 17

## THE ART OF NEGOTIATION - THE 7PS

Employ the 7Ps and you won't go wrong (Proper Planning and Prevention Prevents Piss Poor Performance!)

- **Preparatory steps**
- **General considerations**
- **Having the negotiation**
- **Bad reaction**
- **Good reaction**
- **Example from life**
- **The Negotiation**

## PREPARATORY STEPS

### 1. What is the specific issue you want to change?

Define the issue. Do some thinking about how other issues may interlock with the one you want to resolve (for more on this see the previous chapter, *Finding the Middle Ground (Part 3, Chapter 16)*.

Understand what you are prepared to give, in order to get.

## 2. What are closely related issues that your partner may raise?

Are the reasons your partner might have with your issue credible? Can you see a reason behind the reason which you might be able to point out? You may need an exploratory meeting just to understand what you are up against.

## 3. What change do you want or will you settle for?

Figure out your red lines, sticking points, dotted lines, negotiable and tactical offers.

Understand whether a particular result would please you, satisfy, or be accepted with resignation or resentment?

Examine how you will react to each of those responses and be pragmatic. If they concede, must they do it smiling?

## 4. Why has this arisen now?

Understand your partner's position and reasoning in relation to the division between you. Is the issue in question a long-running difference or a new one? If new, can you see how it evolved in response to a recent change in circumstances? Has it emerged because *your* expectations have changed?

Prepare non-accusing/non-blaming questions to sympathetically understand their point of view. Simply mind-reading or judging from your standpoint is not going to be helpful.

From other discussions previously, you can probably guess how your partner will react. Do they seem to listen but later show they haven't grasped the issue and/or don't intend to change? Do they use an immediate, impatient rejection of the facts?

Their reaction is almost always habitual and predictable. Make sure your negotiating style is under your control and appropriate. See *Keeping calm (Part 1, Chapter 6)* and *Thinking (Part 1, Chapter 3)* for more on this.

## 5. What benefits might your partner gain from the change? What, if necessary could you change, in exchange? Think hard about this one!

Make a list of the potential benefits of the new arrangements to your partner. If they can see an upside, they will be more likely to agree to your request.

## GENERAL CONSIDERATIONS

What is the general mood between you? Warm, close, distant, angry?

Mood music? What have you done recently to show you care? See *Expressing Love (Part 2, Chapter 8)*.

What are you doing to control your own anger? Breath, exercise? See *Keeping Calm (Part 1, Chapter 6)*.

## HAVING THE NEGOTIATION

Now you have done the preparation above, both specific (Preparatory Steps) and general (General Considerations) , it is time to plan for the actual negotiation. Your style during the negotiation must be warm, co-operative, exploratory, willing to listen. Using the phrase, *'I wonder…'* is a helpful way to offer your partner an idea to consider in a neutral way.

Do not allow yourself to assume, mind-read, or employ a demanding, impatient, bullying, whingey, tearful or pleading tone. See *Learning to Listen (Part 2, Chapter 13)*.

*Never* focus on historic grievances. Explore new ways of proceeding. The past is gone. For more on this, see *Forgiveness (Part 4, Chapter 25)*.

Choose **a moment** when neither of you are tired or hungry. Maybe play some relaxed music but don't have screens on and see if you can get your partner to leave their phone next door! Sit side-by-side if possible, preferably close enough to touch.

**Frame** the conversation by starting with a subject of shared interest or warm memories where that still exists between you.

Remembering what you learnt from *Communicating Well (Part 2, Chapter 12)* be sure to present yourself as warm and open, not tense or aggressive. You could set the scene with: *I was thinking about, I came across this photo, I do/did so enjoy...*

What partner behaviour linked to this issue can you praise them for? *I was proud of you when xxx happened and you managed that tricky situation so well...*

The point of 'framing' is to open the way for the partner to identify with the change you seek.


BAD REACTION

**Read this 10 times!**

If at this point your partner is clearly not listening or showing enough interest (signs might include eyes sliding away, an expression of boredom, distracted by a third thing – phone, child, noise outside etc.) **do not get cross**! Breathe deeply! Then say in a concerned voice, *Darling, I am feeling a bit worried about you. Is something bothering you?*

Put your OWN issue to one side for the moment and lovingly, with touch, get the partner to look inwards. If your partner is still uncooperative, say, *I really would like a little talk about why I'm worried about you/ us/the family, but not now is fine.*

This is a tactic. Your partner may then come out with *their* issues. Their lack of cooperation is signalling bigger, deeper problems which will require you to put your issue on the back burner for now and focus on how *they* are feeling.

Try not to feel angry with them for changing the topic under discussion, but see it as progress because they are telling you what they feel matters to them and this is progress! After all, communication is the name of the game!

Never allow just one issue to define the whole relationship. Pull focus and see the bigger picture. There is always a bigger picture!

For more on coping with this, see *Bad Reactions (Part 4, Chapter 22).*

## Good Reaction

If your partner has warmed up after your bonding and praise, it's probably safe to open up your issue.

*Darling I am feeling a bit worried/upset by something, may I share?* (Use the word **share** not tell, to avoid them getting defensive). *Darling I can't understand why, when you are so caring* *generally/on other issues, why you do this or that?* (This expresses puzzlement not accusation).

None of this resolves the problem which will need discussion, give-and-take, and probably some compromise on your part, but the whole point of the conversation is to:

(a) to make your partner realise what their moods/behaviours may be risking/costing them
(b) to get the issue into the open without causing anger and defensive instincts to be aroused

## EXAMPLE FROM LIFE

Katie visits her mother, Penny, frequently. Usually her partner, Mark, goes too, but he would prefer to play golf. Mark is the one wanting change, so it is he who must make a plan. I use the 7Ps to illustrate the method below:

### P1: Mark's point of view

He must evaluate the negative effect on him (and therefore on his relationship) in terms of the time and effort of visiting Grandma Penny so often.

### P2: Katie's point of view

Why does Katie want to go so often to see her mother? Perhaps Grandma Penny is ill, frail, lonely, needs help with this, that or the other?

### P3: What change can Mark settle for?

Could Grandma Penny come to visit *them* more often? Could Katie go alone more often? If she needs assistance, are there other people who could help? Eg. a charity visitor or a cleaner etc.

## P4: Why does Mark want change?

He might have work pressure, and he has taken up a new hobby, golf, which squeezes his time otherwise available for visiting Grandma Penny.

## P5: Is this a long-running difference or new?

Possibly Mark has never liked Penny much and Katie might be aware of this. How will this fact play into the negotiation?

## P6: Mark needs to put himself in Katie's shoes

Perhaps Katie knows Mark doesn't like Penny much and feels angry with him for that. Making him visit her might be the way Katie has chosen to cope with that fact (denial, trying to fit a square peg into a round hole etc.) Mark might be aware that Katie also finds her mother difficult and it might be long-standing emotional issues that prevent Penny and Katie having a more open, honest relationship. Mark might well have been sucked into playing 'Happy Families' up to now. Perhaps he is sick of this (an example of 'the reason behind the reason' which often lurks behind a person's wish for change).

## P7: What benefits might Katie gain from the change? What, if necessary could Mark offer, in exchange?

Perhaps Katie might feel better if she acknowledged how hard she finds her mother to cope with, especially as she ages. It might set Katie free to renegotiate the terms of their relationship which Mark could offer to help her do. If Mark couches it in terms of how he wants to help Katie handle her mother in a better way for her, Mark is more likely to get what he wants. Could he offer to arrange a cleaner for Katie's mother perhaps, in exchange for not having to go?

## THE NEGOTIATION

Here are two options for what Mark could say:

---

**Option 1:** *"Darling Katie* [using an endearment and their name to get their attention] *I've been considering giving up my golf membership as I really can't cope with work pressure and the weekend activities as well as visiting your mum as often as we do.* I feel like *something has to give! Do you think we could make a list of everything we are doing at the weekend and see how we can figure things out so I don't feel so frantic?"*

---

The list will include Katie's mother but also things that Mark values more. By making Katie join in on making the list, the direct assault on her mum is avoided. Arguments for and against various activities are applied to other things before visits to Penny come up, so that when the visits are then discussed, the concept of finding alternative solutions has already been established.

---

*"Yes I understand that she's your mum and I praise you for your devotion to her, but she's not my Mum. I'm not sure that you insisting we all visit Penny so often and that I give up golf is reasonable or fair. Surely you could go on your own once a month and I could come with you once a month. Does that sound reasonable?"*

---

The use of the words *fair* and *reasonable* and *giving up something* makes Katie need to justify her position rather Mark needing to defend *his*.

---

**Option 2:** *"Dearest Katie,* [using an endearment and their name to get their attention] *I've been thinking. You know you said you wish we could have nights away/nights out together more often?*

*I think that's a brilliant idea, let's plan to. A practical problem to solve is how to fit in the time, or find the money. Can we together make a list of what we must give up if we are to do what you say you'd like to do?"*

---

This second approach frames the entire 'change' that Mark wants as an advantage for Katie. Generally speaking, if you can see an upside for the partner in the change you are proposing, that is the best way to persuade them. After all, we are all selfish, self-interested creatures!

## CONCLUSION

Perhaps all this sounds a bit contrived? Why not just be blunt?

---

**Mark:** *"No, I'm not going so often to your effing mother because she is a b**** and I've got better things to do."*

---

Mark may be entirely justified in what he *feels*, but the relationship will not thrive if he *says* exactly what he feels!

Katie's anger will rumble on in moods, sulks, counter-anger and blame. If this sounds familiar, then why not try *Finding the Middle Ground (Part 3, Chapter 16)* and see if your relationship can become a nicer place to live?

You can use this method whenever you find yourself unable to agree. With good will on both sides, there is always a way to find a win/win solution. If your partner sees you are trying to help and support their goals rather than competing or contesting them, a more positive bond will emerge.

Talking, tenderness and employing this method can enable both of you to meet your emotional needs.

## Chapter 18

# Get Your Partner Talking

Unless your partner is in a deep depression which is a medical problem for which they need *professional help* (see *Part 6*), there will be something that they need to talk about but for reasons you don't understand, they don't want to.

There will be things that you used to talk about. You will have *shared* memories and interests. So find some way of introducing a warm, shared subject. Photos of past holidays or memories of happy times will work.

Give your partner the room, space and time to readjust from a tense atmosphere to having a nice time. Don't intrude on them with your worries/preoccupations. Smile. Ask neutral questions. Wait for them to talk.

If you have managed to get onto a cheerful topic, do some praising and tender touching. Try to keep this going, talk about anything, but share it in a light-hearted way.

When your partner has engaged at *some level* for some time and contributed to the conversation at least 3 or more times, then you can then reintroduce your need for change.

## EXAMPLE 1 - I REMEMBER WHEN...

A good way is to start with something like *I really did enjoy it when we went/did xyz. We were so in love then!*

Pause, check you have their eye contact and they are listening. *You know I still love you.*

Then ask any of the following:

- *What are your best memories?*
- *How are you feeling about our relationship currently?*
- *Is our love going wrong?*
- *Can we talk about it?*

Notice the use of 'our' and 'we' in these questions to encourage a sharing, caring state of mind.

## EXAMPLE 2 – MANY WORDS FOR LOVE

Another sideways approach is to say *I have been reading about all the different words for love the ancient Greeks had. Do you want to look at them with me?* Print out *Ancient words for love (Part 2, Chapter 9)* and look at it together. *Which ones apply to us do you think?*

As relationships change, so can the love words.

## EXAMPLE 3 – THE LOVE LANGUAGES

Another way to approach a change conversation might be, *'I never realised that people express and expect love in so many different ways.'* Print out *Expressing love (Part 2, Chapter 8).*

Try to open up these topics in an exploratory rather than bossy way. Treat them as something to share, be curious about and enjoy, rather than topics to tick off your list.

All of this is hard work but it's work for a purpose. The aim is a more hopeful, happy relationship. It's almost certainly worth it. See *From frying pan to fire (Part 5, Chapter 33)* if you are feeling dubious about bothering.

## Chapter 19

# Opening Up a Conversation

The worst time to open a "change" conversation is when you or your partner/child are already angry, hungry, tired or upset. 'H-angry' is a dangerous state!

"*Right, we need to talk*" said in an angry tone, when they are in the middle of a task, sets you up for a battle, not an effort to find joint solutions.

Spend a couple of days prior to the time you hope to talk by setting the scene. Guard your own words and body language by reacting kindly to their moods. Try to find something, anything, that you still share, be it food, photos, music or funny videos, and see if you can draw your joint attention to it.

You want your brains to be in care/share mode, rather than rage/fear mode. What you think about immediately before the talk will determine the tone of your non-verbal communications.

Practice your opening phrases in a mirror to make sure your mind and body are reading from the same hymn sheet. See *Communicating well (Part 2, Chapter 12)* for more on this.

When you have done your best to set the scene, and it's a quiet, private time, you might begin...

Always use your partner's/child's name or an endearment to start.

*Darling* [add their name], *I'm feeling a bit low. I think I'm feeling a bit* [sad/confused/whatever feeling is dominating for you]. *Can we sit and have a quiet word/talk/chat?*

Pause to listen. Your non-blaming words will usually gain your partner's attention. Compare using the above sentence with, '*I'm feeling a bit unloved*', (note the implied criticism) or '*I need to say something*' (note the implied conflict).

Your pause is to judge the other's immediate response. Check that you have their attention/sympathy/concern before saying the next sentence.

Continue with relationship bonding words such as ...

*"We do/did have such fun when..."*

*"Do you remember..."*

*"I would love to get back to that warmth between us"*

*"Perhaps we could have a bit more of ..."*

Although your list of feelings may include sad/hurt/disappointed/ignored, these words, though true, imply blame and may instinctively trigger anger or counter accusations.

It is better to find/remember some good times and build on them. If your quiet approach has worked, it is time to move on to the next part of the conversation, so see the next chapter, *Good Reaction (Part 3, Chapter 20)*.

However, in a difficult relationship you may be met by *Bad Reactions*, other *Difficult Behaviours*, even *Violence* (see *Part 4*). Go to Part 4 to find out how to manage these reactions.

# CHAPTER 20

## GOOD REACTION

Good news! You and your partner/child seem to be in agreement that changes are needed, but the vibe is far from easy and you are both busy.

Writing down a plan will make a difference so this page is about making sure that both parties know what they have agreed to.

Using pen and paper to work out an agreement you can both stick to has more meaning than yet more screen time. Slow, considered handwriting is, in itself, a form of calming down.

Make it formal. Start off with putting down the *date, time and place.*

*We* [write your name] *and* [let your partner/child write their name] *agree that for the next* [7/14 days] *we will make an effort to spend some quality time together* [specify the period of time and the frequency, eg. 30 minutes every other day].

*We agree that could include* [put at least 5 ideas in this box you both agree to].

You can put forward suggestions from the list below or make up your own, obviously.

- Walk in nature
- Garden together
- Plan a meal, shop and cook it together
- Read poems to each other
- Karaoke singing
- Crosswords/sudoko
- Listen to a whole music album together
- Jigsaw puzzles
- Couple yoga
- Give each other a foot massage (15 mins each)
- Learn Indian Head Massage (15 mins each)
- Parlour games (charades, blind man's buff etc.)

Try to make the quality time screen-free where possible, as listening/looking at a screen is not as effective in creating quality time as looking and listening to your partner/child.

---

*On* [put in date 7-14 days from now], *we will sit here together to see how we are getting on. Do we feel better, more optimistic about us? If so, perhaps we will continue this agreement, specifying what we will do and putting in a date for our next check-in.*

*If we don't feel more friendly after this time spent together, let's agree to carry on exploring our difficulties.*

*We agree to end our meetings with loving words and gentle touch.*

*Signed* [you] *and* [your partner/child]

---

What many of us forget is how physical we are, how our brain and body are constantly talking to each other via our vagal nerve, signalling and releasing either feel-safe, feel-good chemicals or stress chemicals depending on what we are feeling in our relationships. This is why turning off your phone and turning up for quality time together is so important. Making the plan can be a bonding exercise in itself.

If the plan didn't work (yet) and relations remain strained, what now? Analyse what went wrong – did you fail to stay in care/share brain mode? Did they? Never mind. Forgive yourself and your partner. Decide to 'fail better' next time.

Winston Churchill's advice is helpful: 'Success is not final. Failure is not fatal. It is the keeping going that counts!'

The following sections might be useful to read (again):

- ***Keeping calm (Part 1, Chapter 6)***
- ***Communicating well (Part 2, Chapter 12)***
- ***Finding the middle ground (Part 3, Chapter 16)***
- ***Opening up a conversation (Part 3, Chapter 19)***

## PART FOUR

# WHEN THE GOING GETS TOUGH

# CHAPTER 21

## MISUNDERSTANDINGS

- **Why misunderstandings happen**
- **Hack your mind**

Words always have more than one meaning and their meaning depends on context, time, place, previous exchanges, intended use etc.

A speaker's choice of words is loaded with the baggage of their own assumptions.

Quite often, what we say is far less than what we are unconsciously implying.

The listener's assumptions and associations may also be quite different.

### WHY MISUNDERSTANDINGS HAPPEN

Misunderstandings mostly happen because a speaker expects their listener to see the same connections they do, and/or to read their mind. We all use words imprecisely; or even worse, we employ the dreaded *'you always/you never'*.

These terms are red rags to a bull because they are always untrue. This is because even if they 'almost always' forget to put the cap on the toothpaste, there will be rare occasions when they did!

Just take the word 'cat'. To you, the word 'cat' might generate associations such as 'cuddly, beautiful, independent, mine'. To your partner, the word 'cat' might conjure: 'costly, yours, pointless, nuisance, hair-depositing, burden'.

Or take 'Sunday', for instance. To one partner it might mean, 'Hobby, relax, Sunday papers, sex, chilling out'. To the other, it could mean 'Housework, gym, mow lawn, wash car'. This couple's unacknowledged assumptions about 'Sunday' could easily produce a row: 'You never just stop and take it easy!' versus 'Why don't you ever do anything useful?'

## HACK YOUR MINDS

When you realise every word you use carries a whole mass of meanings and values, which your partner may not necessarily share, then you can avoid the stress, puzzlement, confusion and anger which may result from talking at cross purposes.

In negotiation or disagreements, whatever nonsense you hear your partner/child utter, it is more useful to pause, show interest and say, *'Yes, there may be some truth in what you are saying'* rather than to hammer out a blanket *'You are wrong!'* or *'No'*.

This is because their brain will unconsciously respond to *'No'* by calling up their inner stubborn toddler (brain scans have shown this). By saying, *'I see what you mean'* even if you don't rather than, *'That is so stupid'*, you will recruit a more reasonable, 'grown-up' part of their brain to join the conversation.

# CHAPTER 22

## BAD REACTIONS

You have tried to open a calm conversation. Your partner/child is not engaging.

You may get various levels of unhelpful response:

- **Avoidance**
- **Anger**
- **Threats to leave**
- **Gaslighting**

### AVOIDANCE

This is a common problem in relationships. Many people have learned from infancy that avoiding conflict is less painful than confronting the fact that your caregiver doesn't seem to care how you feel. This is especially true when it comes to discussing emotional issues.

It is worth bearing in mind that many of us have an angry, hurt and defensive little child inside our unconscious mind (and an actual little child in front of us as parents!) who can make us feel intensely unpleasant emotions (anger, fear, hate). When avoidant behaviour is being used by you or your partner/child, your/their inner child inside them is saying 'Back off!' See *Emotions (Part 1, Chapter 1)* and *Attachment Styles (Part 2, Chapter 14)* for more on this.

Avoidant behaviour happens when you/they are trying to talk about something important and you/they:

- aren't listening
- won't put down their phone
- avoid eye contact
- offer a half-hearted agreement but no firm commitment
- fidget
- get distracted (pick up the TV remote, go to the fridge)

Whatever the historic cause of the avoidant behaviour, it must be tackled in the here and now if it isn't to derail your relationship.

## WHAT TO DO ABOUT IT

If it is you being avoidant, see *Attachment Styles* and do some work on yourself, potentially *seeking professional help* (see *Part 6*). If it is your partner/your child who is being avoidant, first off, keep your cool! Remember, their avoidant behaviour may trigger your own ignored inner child which this is why you need to use these tactics on yourself to *Keep calm (Part 1, Chapter 6)*.

If they are being avoidant, realise that you are dealing with an actual child/your partner's inner child, so use their name a lot to reassure them and use a gentle tone of voice. Hold hands or gently touch them. Turn the occasion into an expression of genuine concern for *them*. Avoid blame or accusation. Don't bring up ancient history, or anything else in the present which is annoying you about them.

Say instead, any of these questions:

- *What are you thinking about?*
- *Are you tired/bored?*
- *Are you worried about us?*
- *Shall we talk about something else?*

All this is non-threatening, non-accusatory and works much better than an exasperated you hissing at them, '*You are not listening!*' in an aggressive tone. Or even worse, throwing at them the dreaded '*You never listen!*'

If you want to *Get your partner talking (Part 3, Chapter 18)* and sharing, you have to turn the whole conversation into your concern for *them*. Remember you are not communicating with their rational, grown-up self when you get an avoidant response, but the scared child who doesn't think you care about how they feel. Keep this fact front and centre of your mind: **they don't feel safe**.

Talking about anything is better than nothing. Listen carefully - they may reveal some hidden pain, grievance or worry. If you are patient, interested, responsive and caring, *not* exasperated, angry or impatient, your partner will (eventually) feel safe enough to talk. This will counter their unconscious expectation that they are not safe. Only once the child has quietened down can their grown-up self come out to play. Then, and only then, can a useful, grown-up conversation begin.

## ANGER

Signs of anger can involve any, or all, of the following:

- aggressive body language (head turned away from you, folded arms, crossed legs)
- angry facial expressions (sneering, frowning, narrowed eyes)
- counter accusations ('Well, you *did* this, that, or the other')
- blame and slander ('You *are* this, that, or the other')
- a contemptuous, sarcastic, belittling tone of voice

## WHAT TO DO ABOUT IT

To quote Yoda from *Star Wars*, "Fear is the path to the dark side. Fear leads to anger. Anger leads to hate. Hate leads to suffering." Try to remember that underneath anger, fear is almost always lurking. Your partner/your child is frightened of something, but they (and you) probably don't know what. They may not realise they even sound angry, contemptuous or sarcastic even though that seems utterly self-evident to you.

Can you wonder out loud if they realise how angry they sound? If they deny it or say, *'No, you are the angry one'*, try saying, *'Yes, you might be right that I am sounding angry or sarcastic. If so, I am really sorry.'*

This has the effect of giving them pause and may offer them an opportunity to reset and apologise for their words/tone. If you *are* angry (and why *wouldn't* you be if they are talking to you in a nasty way) simply denying you are upset and angry puts the conversation straight into a defensive tailspin.

If your partner/child is violent, see *Violence (Part 4, Chapter 27)*.

But if the anger is non-violent:

- Do *not* respond with your own anger. It is *never* helpful to respond with anger to your partner's anger.
- If their anger increases, smile, use their name and say *'I can see you are angry, please sit down and tell me how exactly you think I can do something to help.'*
- If the anger still continues, say again in a "helping" way with appropriate body language and facial expression, *'Your anger puzzles me, can I help?'*
- Don't ask *'Why are you angry?'* as it is too easily seen as a challenge. *'How can I help?'* works much better.

The whole idea is to *change* their mood music.

Angry people want to shout not think; they expect others to shout at them and/or fight back. But angry brains are soon muddled when all your body language, tone of voice and words are emitting *calm, concern, love*.

Since anger is a way to defend against fear, if there is nothing to fear from your body language and tone of voice, their body will begin to calm down.

If none of this works, simply disengage, tell them you think you should leave the conversation until both of you have calmed down (don't say, 'When *you* calm down' as that will antagonise them) and go off to do something else. Don't leave by door-slamming.

If they are blaming and accusing you, see the next chapter on *Being Blamed (Part 4, Chapter 23)*.

## THREATS TO LEAVE

If someone is both angry, avoidant or both, they might:

- Turn up the emotional temperature with counter-blame and accusation.
- Shout at you: *'I can't do this anymore!'*, *'Leave then!'*, *'I'm leaving!'* or *'Why don't you just go and find someone else?'*
- These comments are covert threats to abandon you if you persist in talking about your relationship difficulties.

## WHAT TO DO ABOUT IT

Coping with this behaviour means getting hold of your fear that you will be abandoned by your partner. This understandably activates your own attachment behaviour (see *Attachment Styles, Part 2, Chapter 14*) and without reflection, you will react angrily. So first use the techniques in *Keeping Calm (Part 1, Chapter 6)* and once you have calmed down, understand that your partner only threatens you when *they* feel powerless.

They may have heard your request for change and felt afraid that they will not be able to change, leading them to fear you will leave *them*! Throwing up their arms in despair therefore functions as a diversion tactic designed to evade the need for change. Ask your partner very calmly to consider if they do mean their threat.

If they won't answer this question, say you would like to park the conversation, leave the room (and the row) and go off and do something else that makes you feel good (like having a bath, going for a walk, listening to music you like).

Restart the conversation at the next appropriate time and ask them if they meant the threat. If they say, *'Yes, I meant the threat'*, well at least you now *know* you have a very serious problem on your hands and that the relationship might be ending.

If they say, *'No, I didn't meant the threat'*, then they were trying to intimidate you and behaving like a bully. So you need to calmly point out that they are making empty threats and ask them to continue the important conversation about what in the relationship needs to change.

If they repeat their threat to leave at a later date, point it out calmly, then leave the conversation and come back to it when you are feeling calmer. If this endlessly repeats, then you may need to *Seek professional help (Part 6)*.

## GASLIGHTING

If someone in your relationship does any of the following on a regular basis:

- demands you agree to something you know not to be true
- insists you/they said or did something you/they didn't
- displays irrational jealousy
- claims you are crazy/too sensitive

Then this is gaslighting behaviour. If you/your partner says these things you/they are perpetrating emotional violence. It may not leave physical marks on the body, but the body keeps the score all the same. Being treated this way produces waves of panic, fear, anxiety and/or dread.

Essentially if this is happening to you, your body is saying, '*I am frightened by this person*' but you are dismissing this knowledge in order to preserve a relationship you depend on (for shelter/food/warmth and/or because you feel you can't leave them because of dependents).

When the body's communications are split off from the mind, we feel *shame*. Shame is an ancient defence. It immobilises us because it is trying to keep us safe (like poking a spider until it plays dead). Shame makes us feel we can't tell anyone or leave the relationship and/or get help. This is an awful situation to find ourselves in.

## WHAT TO DO ABOUT IT

If you are the victim of this behaviour, keep reminding yourself, '*It is **not my fault**'* and '*My body never lies'*. This means you can give yourself permission to take your feelings of anger, grief and panic seriously.

Do not delude yourself that you can 'love' your partner/child out of gaslighting behaviour or that they can 'love' you into being common-garden avoidant or angry, if it is you who are gaslighting them. You/your partner *can* change but you *will* need help.

Start by telling someone you trust how about how your partner's destructive behaviour is making you feel. See the chapter on *Coercive Control (Part 4, Chapter 26)* for where to go next.

## A TAKEAWAY

Accusing, blaming and nagging your partner/child *never* works. **Changing habits is difficult.** Getting angry back in a fight triggers their mammalian brain area to release more cortisol and adrenalin to the gut, heart and muscles preparing their body for fight or flight. Neither is needed here. Make sure you are in a good space for difficult discussions by reading the chapter on *Keeping Calm (Part 1, Chapter 6)* then find a good time to try again.

# CHAPTER 23

## BEING BLAMED

If your partner/child is aware that things are not going well or that you are unhappy, then they may employ a common defence, namely to blame you and evade any responsibility for needing to change. Remember, everyone hates change when it is at another's instigation. This includes you *and* your partner!

You must expect this. So, don't blame back. Assume there may be some truth in what's said when they blame you for something.

Arrange a time to sit down together. Frame the conversation with good, shared memories. See *Asking the right questions (Part 3, Chapter 15)*.

Remember how much your tone of voice and body language matter. Control your face to be open, interested and receptive - see *Communicating well (Part 2, Chapter 12)*.

To get your partner/child to state their problem in as precise and clear way as they can, say:

*OK, I'm ready to listen* [Pause, smile at them. Then say]

*Please tell me slowly what you are thinking.* [Really listen, nod, empathise, clarify, don't argue!]

Then feed back to them the exact words of their main criticism(s). Imagine you are a doctor repeating reported symptoms. *OK,* [use their name, recite their criticisms then say] *Have I got that right?* [Pause. Say slowly...making eye contact] *OK, I understand. What are we going to do about it?*

[Then be quiet. Look/act loving and expectant].

This technique takes the heat out of a situation. Your response is unexpected, not blaming back. Using *we* turns the complaint into a shared task. Saying '*What are we going to do* about it' extends the time frame and takes the immediate demand for a solution out of the frame.

## WHAT NEXT?

The secret is to keep being helpful. Never say *That's ridiculous, untrue, nonsense.*

If you don't like what they are proposing, don't say '*No that's a stupid idea*'. Ask, '*Have we considered the cost/time/consequences of* [any given action]'. Ask, '*If we do this, what about that?*'

Or, '*If I change and do this instead, it may effect X, Y or Z. How are we going to deal with that?*''

Obviously, if the complaint is justified, be prepared to change your behaviour! Conclude the talk with '*I'm glad we talked, I'm glad I can help.*' End with a hug.

# Chapter 24

## Difficult Behaviours

Can you name the seven deadly sins? They are pride, greed, lust, envy, gluttony, wrath and sloth. I bet you are guilty of at least a few on a regular basis. I know I am!

In *Emotions (Part 1, Chapter 1)* we covered the two basic drives of **survival** and **reproduction**. It is true to say a great deal of 'sinful' behaviour follows from these drives. An evolutionary psychologist might argue prideful behaviour is a display of your fitness to mate; while gluttony, in the hunter-gatherer environment in which humans evolved, actually makes a lot of sense when you might only find honey once a year!

But these days most of us don't live in a state of nature and in fact, our modern, Western society is turning out to be rather bad for us given the rise in 'mismatch' health conditions such as depression, anxiety, heart failure, obesity and diabetes.

Cleverer people than me have researched why too much choice leads to depression and feelings of loneliness (see *Other*

*Resources* in *Part 6* for more on this). The truth is we are paying for our increased affluence and freedom with a substantial decrease in the quality and quantity of community.

What was once given by family, neighbourhood and workplace must be bought by the individual from their (often too meagre) earnings. Think for example of nursery care for the under 5s or the cost of a live-in carer for an aged relative. The social fabric which holds us together at our vulnerable ages is no longer a birthright of community-based living, but a series of deliberate and demanding consumer choices.

Modern consumerism requires advertisers to convince us that, 'We are what we buy, own, display' while social media companies gobble up our precious leisure time persuading us that the image we project to the internet matters more than smelling a rose or appreciating the trill of a robin. Our society's set up means we work too hard, borrow too much and thus get ill rather than happier.

If you feel that your partner or child is risking the relationship through enacting any of the seven deadly sins, try to turn facing the problem into a shared task. First arm yourself by reading the sections in *Parts 3 & 4* on *Asking the right questions*, *Opening up a conversation*, *Being blamed* and *Bad reactions*.

Common examples of relationship strife might be them spending too much money on things they don't need (greed), refusing to pull their weight financially (sloth), binge-eating on crap their body doesn't need (gluttony), insisting on buying a more expensive house/car/holiday than you can realistically afford because your neighbour has one (envy).

There is always something in the news or a magazine article which will bear down on your issue. Scandals and bad behaviour are eagerly reported! Try using a story in the media to contrive a way to jointly discuss the problem by focusing on a third party. Say *Did you see this article?*

You are not finding these items to prove you are right. The objective is to start thinking of their issue (one of the 7 deadly sins which impacts on you both negatively) in a non-personal, non-blaming way. Try to discover what basic emotion (fear, rage, shame, loneliness, a sense of neglect) is generating your/their difficult behaviours.

Most bad behaviour coming from you/your partner/your child will be caused by you/them feeling unloved and unseen because it is the scared inner child talking from long ago. Can you work out what that child is *saying* through their unhelpful behaviour?

See whether together you can figure out what the triggers might be for the craving/compulsive behaviour and then you might be able to find a way to stop it.

In many cases, *wrath* can be overcome by loyalty, kind words and devotion; *envy* by admiration of their qualities; *sloth* by helping them stick to a plan for bringing about change.

Dopamine, the neurotransmitter released when we find something rewarding, is activated by small achievements — eg. saying you will walk to the shops every day and actually doing it, rather than making grand plans to run the Marathon next year. Talking things through will reassure them, helping them feel they are not alone.

The skill, as ever, is not to blame, accuse or deny the feelings but to help them meet their emotionally-driven needs in more helpful ways.

If you/your partner/your child may be suffering from a diagnosable mental health condition such as violent behaviour, gambling addiction and/or substance misuse, it makes sense to Seek professional help (see Part 6). There is nothing weak about asking for help.

# CHAPTER 25

## SAYING SORRY

- **Making mistakes**
- **What to do about it**
- **When to compromise**
- **The art of saying sorry!**

### MAKING MISTAKES

'Forgive and forget'. If only this were as easy to do as it is to say!

Humans make mistakes. Saying sorry matters.

Sometimes the mistake harms the doer, sometimes it harms others. We can make mistakes of omission (not doing something) or mistakes of commission (doing something).

The doer's intention matters. We all know we can forgive an oversight more easily than a deliberate act of aggression (or greed). Then there is well-intentioned harm, such as buying chocolates as a present for someone trying to diet.

The degree of harm matters, too. Forgetting an anniversary is bad but crashing the car while drunk-driving is much worse! Guilt (a willingness to take responsibility for harm done) and the ability to say sorry varies between individuals. Some find acts of reparation very difficult especially if they are afflicted with low self-esteem and struggle with their *Emotions (Part 1, Chapter 1)*.

We need to distinguish between physical or financial harm which is often measurable and for which some kind of recompense is negotiable; and actions, either real or imagined, that cause offence (usually ego-bruising) to another person.

It is more often this latter harm which breeds resentment in relationships. Clearly if we cause physical, financial or emotional harm, the onus falls on us, the doer, to apologise and make good. That is easier said than done and we are all tempted to make excuses for ourselves.

What about the person harmed? The Science is clear (just Google 'resentment and health'). Put simply, carrying around resentment is like drinking poison hoping to harm another. Whether resentment is based on envy, anger or fear, it is definitely bad for you.

## What to do about it

First identify what you are resentful about. Is it a particular event(s) located in the past or a continuing behaviour?

Now ask yourself what you want. Do you want your feelings about X, Y or Z to be respected? Do you want an apology, reparations and/or to stop a current behaviour?

Now we have some answers, we have done our preparation. Now it is time to *Open up a conversation (Part 3, Chapter 19)*. It might help to read the section on *Asking the right questions (Part 3, Chapter 15)* too.

Once you've had the conversation, if your partner or child feels very strongly that your resentment is still unreasonable, you must ask yourself the following questions:

1. Have I checked with a third party (friend, relative) to see if my resentment is reasonable?
2. Am I resentful on behalf of someone else (eg. your child)
3. If so, is what I am worried about something that actually happened to me when *I* was a child? Could I be siphoning off into my child the feelings *I* feel somewhere deep inside that I haven't properly dealt with? If you can identify these, talk about them with your partner. If you are mystified, see if they can help you figure it out. If you both don't have a clue, think about *Seeking professional help (Part 6)*.

A nugget of wisdom offered by my 15-year old daughter, when we were discussing the issue of resentment for this book was: 'Mum, if you don't care about who you are blaming, then scapegoating works. But if you do, then you are making someone you love feel bad. And because you love them, you are making yourself feel bad as well. So it really doesn't work!'

Living in resentment is no way to live.

## When to compromise

All relationships involve give and take, negotiation and compromise. If (in a calm and reasonable fashion) you have made your partner or child aware that a particular behaviour causes you emotional distress and you have asked them kindly to desist and they don't, what should you do?

For the sake of your relationship, you may decide to overlook small annoyances (leaving the toilet seat up, the cap off the toothpaste, stacking the dishwasher in a gormless way, leaving their room messy etc.) or to forgive them for an historic event.

To help yourself do this, ask yourself, *'In the bigger scheme of things, does it really matter?'* Or *'Will I be lying on my deathbed feeling annoyed about this issue?'*

If the answer is yes, and the behaviour continues with the offender both defiant and dismissive of your feelings (see Coercive Control), then 'forgiving' or rather, failing to forgive and carrying round lots of resentment, is likely to do you more harm to you than good. In this circumstance, you might need to *Seek professional help (Part 6).*

## The art of saying sorry

I apologise if this sounds very basic, but it seems worth reiterating that a true apology is composed of five different elements:

1. Ownership - *'Yes, I did do/say X or Y'*
2. Empathy - *'I can see it made you feel A and B'*
3. Expression of regret - *'I am sorry'*, no ifs, no buts!

4. Restitution - a gift/present of time to try to repair things
5. A plan of how you will avoid doing it again.

Saying sorry can feel really difficult. It can stick in all our throats, but a proper sorry goes a long way to resolving tension in a relationship. It isn't a proper sorry though, if your 'verbals' (what you say) don't match your 'non-verbals' (your facial expression and body language).

Muttering 'Sorry' under your breath or shouting 'Sorry' and flouncing out of the room definitely doesn't count as a proper sorry!

# CHAPTER 26

## COERCIVE CONTROL

- **What is coercive control?**
- **What does it feel like?**
- **How do you spot the behaviours?**
- **How it harms you**
- **How to get out**

### WHAT IS COERCIVE CONTROL?

Controlling or coercive behaviour became a punishable offence in the UK in 2021. It is a form of domestic abuse which is hard to spot if you don't live in the home and experience it, as it is far more psychological than physical.

The phrase 'coercive control' was coined by Evan Stark whose book *Coercive Control: How Men Entrap Women in Everyday Life* was published in 2006. According to Stark, "It is a pattern of behaviour which seeks to take away the victim's liberty or freedom, to strip away their sense of self. It is not just a person's bodily integrity which is violated, but also their human rights". Gaslighting is a form of coercive control.

## WHAT DOES IT FEEL LIKE?

You feel constantly monitored, criticized and undermined. There is an unknowable 'rule-book' which is unpredictable and ever-changing. It is like living on shifting sands and you constantly 'walk on eggshells' in case you have done something to 'set them off'. *Fear is central*. Similar to being taken hostage, you become captive in an unreal world created by your abuser, trapped in a world of confusion and contradiction. You come to feel your abuser is all-powerful.

## HOW TO SPOT THE BEHAVIOURS

If your partner engages in *any* of the following behaviours, you have every right to demand they find support to change their ways, or to leave them:

1. Isolating you from your *support system* eg. telling you that friends/family hate you, monitoring your calls, telling lies about you;
2. Keeping you under *surveillance* eg. insisting you share phone/email passwords, installing cameras/recording/spyware devices to watch you;
3. Denying you *freedom* and autonomy eg. not letting you work, stalking you while you are out, taking your phone;
4. *Gaslighting* eg. telling you in the morning they wanted lasagna for dinner, then when you serve it, screaming at you for not giving them burgers because, 'They told you so this morning'. You end up apologising and then wonder, 'Am I going mad?';

5. *Name-calling* eg. using swear words to tell you how deficient and unimportant you are, putting you down, undermining you;

6. Limiting your access to *money* eg. hiding your shared financial resources/information, limiting bank cards, making you live on a very strict budget;

7. Reinforcing traditional *gender roles* eg. if the abuser is male, he might use 'woman as homemaker' to make you do all the cooking, cleaning and childcare;

8. Turning your *kids against you* eg. belittling you in front of them, making them take sides against you;

9. Controlling aspects of your *health and body* eg. telling you how much to eat and sleep, controlling your medications and/or access to healthcare;

10. Making jealous accusations about who you see and when, the better to control your time away from them;

11. Regulating your *sexual relationship* eg. insisting on how much sex you have with them, refusing to use birth control, insisting on making you watch porn or take pictures/videos against your will;

12. *Threatening* loved ones eg. physically threatening pets/children, saying they will call Social Services on you, making decisions about your kids without you agreeing.

## HOW COERCIVE CONTROL HARMS YOU

Unfortunately, living in a coercively controlling relationship has enormous negative consequences. They can be:

- *Physical* effects - bruises, cuts, broken bones, lost teeth, STDs, tiredness due to sleep deprivation.

- Chronic *health* problems - asthma, epilepsy, digestive problems, migraine, hypertension, and skin disorders.
- *Mental health* problems - anxiety, depression, loss of self-esteem, even PTSD, which can lead to negative coping strategies such as reliance on alcohol, medication or self-harm.
- *Social* problems - loneliness, losing jobs and income, struggling to trust or develop relationships, questioning your parenting skills.

## HOW TO GET OUT

You **can** leave an abuser, no matter how long you have been in the relationship. But you need to plan:

1. Maintain *contact* with friends and family, even if you need to get another phone and keep it somewhere secret. Check in regularly with them.
2. Call a domestic violence *hotline* to consult a professional who can help you.
3. *Practice* how to get out safely and practice often. Teach your kids to identify a safe place and train them to reach it and how to call the police.
4. Have a *safety* plan. Abusers are at their most desperate when they are being left (ultimately their behaviour is caused by their own traumatised inner child so they are extremely vulnerable to feeling abandoned). Make sure you can't be found when you do decide to go. See *Self-protection* and *Violence (Part 4, Chapters 27 & 28)* for more on this.

## CHAPTER 27

## VIOLENCE

- **What to do if your partner is violent**
- **What if you are the violent one?**

According to the Office for National Statistics, roughly 1 in 30 people in the UK are in abusive relationships. If that is you, do not despair. Remember that inside every perpetrator of violence there is a victim and inside every victim there is a perpetrator. This is most likely because you or your partner grew up in a home where emotional problems were 'solved' by violence. This is what was modelled and so this is what you/they do now.

If you have children observing/experiencing violence in their home, you will be making new perpetrators/victims who will make their future family lives a misery. What you need to understand is that children witnessing or hearing a terrible fight is emotional abuse to the children, not just unpleasant for the adults. It doesn't have to be this way. You can be the one who breaks the cycle. It is essential to *Seek professional help (Part 6)*.

This book is about action, not theory. If the violence is really serious, you must get outside help. But read *Self-protection (Part 4, Chapter 28)* to make yourself safer if you are, or might become, the victim of domestic violence.

## WHAT TO DO IF YOUR PARTNER IS VIOLENT

- **Learn from the pattern.**
- **Note the times, the triggers.**
- **Anticipate the behaviour.**
- **Calm yourself by breathing**

If the abuse is emotional (ie. verbal/tone of voice/body language rather than actually physical) see *Coercive control (Part 4, Chapter 26)*.

The key message to remember is that your partner can choose <u>not</u> to act the way they do.

At a time when your partner is **not** angry say '[Their name], *you upset me last night, all that shouting. I have taken professional advice and there's lots I can do* legally' [PAUSE, let that sink in] *'There's also lots you can do to deal with your anger'* [PAUSE, let that sink in] *'Do you want to talk about it?'*

If they get angry and you are scared, take the steps advocated in the next chapter, *Self-protection (Part 4, Chapter 28)*.

## WHAT IF YOU ARE THE VIOLENT ONE?

If you are the abuser, then you will struggle to control your anger at times. When this happens, you might find yourself:

1. Shouting a lot, in a threatening and angry way which reduces your partner/children to tears.
2. Employing coercive control techniques including gas-lighting them.
3. Leaving physical marks on your partner/children after assaulting them or making them hold stress positions.

It is hard to seek help. But many abusers discover that having someone outside the relationship who knows just how intense you can feel at certain moments can make all the difference at the crucial moment.

So can you talk to a friend you trust and tell them how you find yourself behaving? Then when you get really triggered, could you simply walk away and call them instead? Or sit down with a pen and paper and write down how angry you are feeling instead of acting it out? See *Keeping Calm (Part 1, Chapter 6)* for more on this.

You probably feel really ashamed of how you behave after you have been violent and of course you fear that any change in the status quo will result in your partner leaving you/you losing your children.

You might really believe that next time you will be able to control yourself and have promised your partner multiple times that it won't happen again. But then it always does.

The problem is that anger activates circuits in your mammalian (limbic) brain and shuts off contact with your thinking brain (the prefrontal cortex). So no matter how much you want to stop, in the heat of the moment you won't be able to, <u>unless</u> you find new ways of coping with your emotions.

You learnt the habits you already have in response to you not experiencing good-enough care when you were little. These patterns are stored unconsciously and non-verbally deep inside you. See *Attachment Styles (Part 2, Chapter 14)* for more on this. Relying on rational thought and/or wishing to be a better person won't stop the old patterns playing out.

Violence rarely goes away on its own and usually it gets worse. The good news is that plenty of people have been able to change their ways and become more loving, healthier partners and parents. So why not decide to break the cycle of violence and be the change you want to see?

Sit quietly with your partner and go through every step of every page of this book. Pay particular attention to the sections on *Your anger (Part 1, Chapter 7)*. There's a reason for your behaviour. You are *not mad* and you are *not bad*. It is probably a lot to do with the anger/humiliation/shame you felt at being victimised by the perpetrator(s) who hurt you when you were too young to protect yourself/those you loved.

Find these memories and get in touch with the feelings you may have minimised, dismissed or buried somewhere deep inside you. To help you do this, look at childhood photos, visit the places you grew up in, talk to childhood friends or siblings who also witnessed the bad stuff. Grieve for the childhood you didn't have, for the parents who didn't love you well enough. Make a start by working through the Attachment Worksheet from Attachment Styles (Part 2, Chapter 14).

When you learn to treat your inner child with kindness and not hostility, you won't feel so compelled to treat your closest intimates with hostility either. Then think about what triggers your violence and put in place plans for what you can do when you start to feel overwhelmed (see *Keeping calm, Part 1, Chapter 6*). Once you understand the behaviours, you <u>can</u> change them.

This is hard graft to do alone. If you do want to work it through with your partner, set a special time of the week to talk about these horrid memories and give yourself time afterwards to take stock quietly, on your own. Or *Seek professional help (Part 6)*. You could start by enrolling yourself on a Change Project course (www.thechange-project.org).

## Chapter 28

# Self-Protection

This chapter is not about getting into a fight. It is about:-

- **Anticipation**
- **Get out of range**
- **Once safe behind a door**
- **Rape alarms**

### Anticipation

Domestic violence is predictable. On the first signs of trouble (shouting tone, agitation, red-in-the-face, clenched fists) the very worst thing to do is commonly what we *do* do, which is stand face-to-face, toe-to-toe with them. This makes you a sitting duck for their aggression.

### Get Out of Range

If they are in a threatening position, close enough to touch you, Say, '*Oh there it is*' and pretend to pick something up from behind a chair. Start tidying but keep a chair between you and them. '*Hey, I've something to show you, I'll fetch it!*' Go into any room with an inward opening door, keep talking in a friendly way, but shut the door and put a simple wooden door wedge under the door (put them in a useful place inside every room you might need to escape to).

## ONCE SAFE BEHIND A DOOR

Calm yourself down by doing the breathing technique in *Keeping calm (Part 1, Chapter 6)* and talk calmly to them. Use their name or an endearment. Say, '*Dear* [their name] *I can see you are angry, please make a tea, come back and sit down so you can explain to me exactly what you are angry about. I want to help.*'

If you have talked in the past about wanting to help them avoid being violent, remind them of that conversation and say, '*I am here to help, we can keep talking, but I need to stay behind the door just for now.*' That way, you won't activate their inner child to feel abandoned, which could escalate their aggression.

## RAPE ALARMS

Hold 140 decibels close to anyone's ear and they will let go because it hurts. Several rape alarms hidden around the home will enable you to alert neighbours.

You can buy ones that link directly to police stations. Buy several rape alarms and hide them in key places. Order online, get them delivered to a friend/neighbour/office. There are rape alarms that sound like screaming.

As a first step, show the abusive partner that you have **an** alarm (don't mention several) and tell them you've alerted neighbours, the police etc. Keep one alarm near an outside door so you can summon help if you are leaving the house and are scared of being pursued.

Bullies are usually cowards and (if not drunk) can be scared into listening and changing, if you show that you've had enough and will get the Police or Social Services involved.

Remember, the vast majority of people killed in the U.K. each year know their attacker. You are **most at risk** if you have threatened to leave or are actually leaving (the perpetrator's inner child fears the total abandonment and can react violently).

If you are planning to get out, have a refuge set up in advance, don't keep any messages about your plan which they could find on your phone and leave when they are not expecting it.

Continuing to put up with violence is your choice. You *can* stop it, but beware that it can take a bit of time before you are ready to leave. Expect it to be a process not a switch, but get yourself ready mentally to do it.

Many people stay in coercive relationships because their partner tells them, *'You are my saviour'*. This is a fantasy which flatters your ego but it isn't true. You can still pity them without sharing their bed, washing their socks or being their punch bag!

This book is about improving relationships, but if you tolerate, even expect/incite the violence, then *Seek professional help (Part 6)*, especially if there are children involved, because you are emotionally abusing your children by turning them into your witnesses and the cycle of abuse is being passed on to the next generation. See *Other Resources (Part 6)* for more info.

# PART FIVE

## COMMON PROBLEMS

# CHAPTER 29

## BED DEATH

What defines your 'couple' is that you advertise to the outside world that you have sex (even if you actually don't!) But intimacy can mean very different things to each couple and even within a couple. To one it might mean penetrative intercourse, to another it might mean stroking their hair and giving them a cuddle in the morning. Sexual intimacy is by definition 'done' rather than spoken about. But when issues arise in the bedroom, talking really is our only way through.

Asking your partner about intimacy and what it signifies to them is really important and you might be surprised by their answers. Obviously enjoying physical intimacy is a fast-track to feeling better about your relationship, but if you are not having any intimacy then there are almost certainly other issues in the way.

Let's start with our assumptions about sex. Which *oughts* are in operation for you? (See *Thinking - Part 1, Chapter 3*). Can you have a conversation with your partner about their *oughts* and see where the mismatch might be hiding?

Many men feel that a partner who will have sex with them illustrates that they are 'safe' in the relationship, ie. that they are 'loved'. Many women might think their partner emptying the dishwasher/doing the washing-up illustrates that instead! Understand what sex means to each of us and we can start to see how we may be confusing one thing for another.

Communication really is key. For example, Ben believes if Andrea really loved him, she would always be the one to initiate sex despite them having been married for many years.

Andrea enjoys the sex between them when it happens, but feels they need quality time together first, in order to feel connected enough to want sex with Ben. She thinks Ben ought to be responsible for planning quality time together, not just her, as it historically has been. Their different, unstated beliefs have produced a saddening 'bed death'.

The solution? A frank conversation about their different *oughts* reveals a beneficial *is*. Ben's *ought* is, 'You should initiate sex to show you want me', and Andrea's *ought* is, 'You should make plans for us to spend quality time together'. By expressing their *oughts* as wishes to one another, they both decide to be responsible for initiating sex *and* for making plans for quality time together. They start doing that and hey presto! They start having sex again.

This is such a common situation that if you are dissatisfied with your sex life, it is almost certainly because you are not enjoying enough *Quality time (Part 2, Chapter 11)* with your partner. One, or, more likely, both of you, feel taken for granted and under-appreciated. Use the *Feelings* page *(Part 1, Chapter 2)* to work out what the problems are, then read *The art of negotiation (Part 3, Chapter 17)* to devise a way of solving them.

Love is a *doing* verb. How are you and your partner *doing* love? Have a read of ways of *Expressing love* and the *Ancient words for love (Part 2, Chapter 8 & 9)* to see where you might be missing a trick. Finally, remember there are many ways of feeling close to your partner and only you know if sexual intercourse plays a crucial role for you both. Don't be too swayed by the messages the world sends about sex. It is feeling **connected** and close to your partner that is good for your mental and physical health, not only, or necessarily, orgasms.

Esther Perel's website is an excellent resource for imaginative ways to welcome some erotic intelligence into your life. There are more links to explore in *Other Resources (Part 6)* – see Sexual Issues.

## CHAPTER 30

## BETRAYAL

Betrayal can unfortunately take many forms - extramarital romantic liaisons, substance abuse and/or ongoing emotional, physical or sexual abuse. What all these behaviours have in common is that they violate the trust one partner has in the other and this almost always produces trauma reactions.

- Affairs
- Intimidating Behaviour
- Substance Misuse

### AFFAIRS

Trauma reactions if you have been betrayed might well include intrusive and/or circular thought loops, repetitive questioning of your partner about how, what and where they were when they engaged in the betrayal, and/or experiencing strong waves of emotion - anger, sadness, fear - which seem to come and go without obvious cause.

Unless your betraying partner is prepared to end the betraying behaviour, then no healing can happen and the relationship needs space and a period of separation to think about what to do next.

It is a sad fact that the best prediction of future behaviour is past behaviour, so if your partner has promised to change their hurtful behaviour in the past - perhaps many times - but hasn't managed to do so, it is likely that they will fail to change. Parting from them may be the best way to avoid being hurt again.

But let's assume *you* have done the betraying and you *really* do want to change. It can help if you make a daily commitment to apologising. Try saying something like, "*I realise that your thoughts and feelings about what I did might be going round your head during the day and I am really sorry that this is happening to you. I would like to reiterate how committed I am to putting you first and not hurting you again.*"

Apologising is critical (see *Saying Sorry (Part 4, Chapter 25)*) and it isn't possible to over-apologise. You have to show you take full responsibility for the suffering you have caused your partner. If you did have an affair, your partner might be relentless in their questioning about it all. *You* might think they would be better off not knowing and might feel reluctant to give them the gory details, or even start getting annoyed with them for repeatedly asking you about it.

But a way of making sense of traumatic events is to gather information and the discovery of your affair is a traumatic event for your partner. So, above all be patient and answer all their questions as truthfully as you can. Couples *can* get over an affair and relationships can end up stronger because of it.

Some couple therapy sessions might also be helpful to work it all through, not least because difficult conversations can be parked in the therapist's consulting room from week to week. If you end up getting stuck on a particular issue in between sessions, you can agree to park it and take it to the therapist to think about it the following week. See *Seeking Professional Help (Part 6: Other Resources)* for how to find someone to talk to.

## INTIMIDATING BEHAVIOUR

If your partner says they are sorry for being abusive, in whatever form that takes, but then tries to justify themselves with phrases like, '*Well, you did wind me up when you said/did X or Y*', then they do not understand the seriousness of their problems and you should signpost them towards individual therapy and think seriously about leaving the relationship. See *Coercive Control (Part 4, Chapter 26)* for more on this, as well as the chapters on *Violence (Part 4, Chapter 27)* and *Self-Protection (Part 4, Chapter 28)*.

## SUBSTANCE MISUSE

If your partner has a substance misuse problem and has promised to change their behaviour but hasn't already done so, then they are unlikely to fulfil that promise in the future without engaging in a 12-Step programme like AA. If they refuse to do so, then you are signing up for more of the same. If this is untenable, you will have to leave the relationship.

If they are an addict and either of your parents were also addicts, you should probably consider joining an Al-Anon group to help you become wiser about how you play your part in their addictive behaviour patterns. See *Other Resources (Part 6, Chapter 39)* for more info.

# Chapter 31

## Along Comes Baby

Many couples hit the proverbial rocks when they have kids. You know the old adage, 'Two's company, three's a crowd'? Well, for the non child-bearing partner, the bond between the primary caregiver and the baby can make them feel a bit, well, redundant.

When this happens, much older feelings belonging to childhood may come back, triggering powerful feelings of envy and jealousy. This is why it isn't all that unusual for men to start fantasising about other women, or actually engaging in an affair when their partners get pregnant or soon after the birth of their child. Some partners may even become violent for the first time if they had very difficult childhoods (see *Attachment Styles - Part 2, Chapter 14*).

Commonly after childbirth, sexual intimacy doesn't feel like a priority for either (or both parties) as the care of the newborn takes so much time and attention and everyone involved is totally knackered!

So expect the early months of a newborn's life to be a very delicate time for the couple relationship. Like all sensitive periods in a couple's life, it is when communication really matters. It can help to talk about the changes that have happened since the baby's birth.

Some conversation starters could include:

---

*"Having a baby is amazing in loads of ways but are there things you miss about our old life? I know I miss having lazy weekend lie-ins and breakfast in bed…"*

---

Note how using the word *we* signifies your care and concern for 'us', ie. the couple relationship. Or you might say:

---

*"I have been reading about how many people stray when their partner is pregnant or has a baby. I can imagine why that might be so, eg. it might feel like the baby gets priority access over me right now because they are so helpless and needy. I am not implying you are straying, just curious about how it might feel for your inner child right now. If I were him/her, I might be feeling a bit needy and neglected…"*

---

You might follow this up with an idea for how you could spend a few hours together *without* the baby to remind yourselves of the pleasure in being two adults alone.

The British psychoanalyst and paediatrician, Donald Winnicott, wrote a famous paper you can read in *Other Resources (Part 6)*. He lists *18 reasons why parents can hate their babies*. Have a read and see what things you identify with.

Can you share it with your partner and ask them about any negative feelings they have got swooshing around inside them? Society puts a great deal of pressure on parents to feel positive about the experience. But joy isn't the only thing our babies make us feel.

The truth, as every parent knows, is that parenting sometimes feels the absolute opposite of joy. Talking about upsetting or shameful feelings we have as parents with our partner is really liberating.

Remember when you were a kid and you lay in bed seeing scary shadow monsters on the wall, then you plucked up the courage to turn on a light and saw it was nothing but the shape your clothes made hanging over the back of the chair?

Negative feelings (and moods) lessen and may even evaporate when they are shared and met with understanding. Then it becomes possible to use humour to cope with difficult and negative feelings rather than feel guilty and alone with them.

After things settle down a few months in (unless you are a single parent) one of you has probably gone back to work, while the other takes over the majority of the emotional and physical labour of caring for the baby. This is often a particular shock for the partner now staying at home, especially if they were used to earning their own money in the world of grown-ups and now spend their time ministering to His/Her Majesty the Baby.

When kids enter the frame, friction between a couple about division of labour often comes to the fore. The burden of caring for another human being is enormous but it is wage-less work which our consumer society does not value in financial terms. Very often, this falls along gendered lines with the woman at home and the man at work.

A new baby is *unbelievably helpless* – just imagine not being able to so much as roll from your back to your front for the first five months of your life! The enormous work of meeting a dependent baby's needs means the caregiving parent has no choice but to depend on their partner for financial and emotional support.

Then the working partner must shoulder the dependence of both caregiving parent and baby on *their* shoulders, while carrying on meeting the demands of working life. It is a lot and it is no wonder having a baby can hit a couple like a train.

I think it is helpful to imagine that having a baby is a bit like having put you and your partner in harness to pull a heavy wagon on which the baby lies (in idle splendour!) You both do essential but different work to move the wagon forward and neither could manage without the contribution of the other.

Remembering this is helpful because it can avoid common resentments about how uniquely burdened each parent feels. The truth is, you are *both* deeply burdened, but in different ways. Respecting each other's contribution is essential to avoid bad feeling festering between you.

So how to avoid a train wreck?

- Having a baby involves profound identity shifts for both parents, but especially from the person who stays at home to care for the baby. Try to have regular check-ins about what that shift feels like and make space for you both to mourn the lives you had, while acknowledging the new pleasures family life has brought.

- One of the major shifts in identity comes from a change in financial power where the caregiving parent gives up his/her earning power (for a while anyway) and the other partner takes on all the earning responsibilities. Try to talk together about how this makes you feel, from both sides of that divide.

- Try to organise your time so that at least once a week, both parents get time on their own to do something they enjoy *and* time as a couple without the kid(s) around. That way, it won't feel like everything has been given up for the sake of only pulling the wagon.

- If resentment is brewing (eg. it feels like one parent behaves selfishly, while the other is bent under by the work of childcare/domestic work), then you are not pulling the wagon in the same direction. Try to put your finger on the moments when that feels most acute. See *Feelings (Part 1, Chapter 2)* for how to identity what you need to change and how. Then see *Get your partner talking* and *Opening up a conversation (Part 3, Chapter 18 & 19)* for pointers on how to prepare a conversation to change the direction of travel.

- Finally, a word of warning. Sometimes, the primary caregiver can end up being very controlling about how the other partner deals with the baby. This is undermining and unhelpful for all concerned. If they put the nappy on backwards now and then, does it really matter in the bigger scheme of things? What matters is your baby and partner are bonding so unless the baby is screaming their head off, just let your partner get on with it. Be encouraging, praise them and express gratitude - no matter how shoddily you think they may have done the job!

# CHAPTER 32

## MONEY WORRIES

This page makes psychological points, not political ones, but please bear in mind that the consumer society we live in manipulates us to feel needy, discontented and edgy to make us spend money on stuff we don't need in order to soothe ourselves. Many couples fight over money. Who should spend how much, on what?

- **Anxiety and £££**
- **Gambling Issues**
- **Shopping Issues**
- **Some Context**

Every relationship involves three participants, you, your partner and the relationship itself. This third thing – the relationship - has rights of its own. It makes demands on both you and your partner. Let's assume you and your partner had a child, or a pet, or a business together. It goes without saying that you would both have to make sacrifices to enable the child/pet/business to thrive.

It is worth asking yourself when you make a purchase, who is that purchase serving? You, your partner, the relationship? Obviously, you want to have a good balance so that all three dimensions have a chance at getting their needs met. Given money is a limited resource, taking turns seems essential.

Can you identify the purchases (beyond the necessities) over the course of a month and label each purchase as belonging either to you, your partner or the relationship? Having done that, can you see whether the balance is evenly split between the three of you?

## ANXIETY AND £££

When money raises its ugly head in a relationship, it can be very anxiety-making. It is a truism that if you don't have enough money to meet your basic needs, then either you need to spend less or you need to earn more. As Dickens famously had Mr Micawber say in *David Copperfield*, "Annual income twenty pounds, annual expenditure nineteen nineteen and six, result happiness. Annual income twenty pounds, annual expenditure twenty pounds nought and six, result misery." Is it possible to sit down and have a grown-up conversation about how to balance your books?

If this conversation has gone wrong in the past, can you write down the ways in which the conversation goes wrong? Once you have done that, can you put that piece of paper between you and your partner and point out that having this conversation goes wrong in those particular ways and see if you can figure out *together* a different way to go? If you can't, then perhaps a session or two with an independent third party might help. Someone you both trust who you wouldn't want to fight in front of...

Sometimes, one partner feels terrified of going into debt/being in debt, while the other is more relaxed about it and this can often be traced back to childhood experiences of financial pressure/debt problems. This can lead the more financially-anxious partner to feel very let down. The conversation can end up focusing on the practicalities of what has been spent, while the free-floating anxiety often ends up unnamed and therefore unaddressed.

In such cases, a frank conversation about how your anxiety is stirred by money worries is essential to resolve the problem. If your partner is not interested in your anxiety, then ask yourself, *'Is my anxiety over the top?'* Ask a third party (a friend/mentor) to see if they think your anxiety is justified. If they do, then explain calmly to your partner that you don't feel they are taking care of you very well if they cannot take your anxiety seriously. Explain this is a serious problem as it makes you feel they are not worthy of your care and attention so the relationship is at risk.

## GAMBLING ISSUES

What if your partner is a gambler and keeps their expenditure secret? Well, obviously you can't do anything about expenditure you don't know about, but once it becomes evident, then you need to point out their compulsive behaviour has a meaning and they will need to get some help to understand what underlies it so they can choose to behave differently.

There is lots of help out there but like with any problem, they need to acknowledge they have work to do on themselves and if they don't/won't, you have a right to walk away from the relationship. This is because their expenditure stacks up in their 'me' column at the expense of you and most importantly, at the expense of the relationship.

## SHOPPING ISSUES

So, you worry you are a compulsive shopper?

How about the next time you feel the urge to buy something, you ask yourself, *'Why do I want it?'* Sit as quietly as you can (screens off, doors closed) and try to identify which inner voice or outer opinion is driving your certainty that you 'need' it. Or if you are out shopping and you make an impulse-purchase, then remember you don't have to keep it. Keep that receipt and take it back!

How good are you at distinguishing between your needs and your wants?

## SOME CONTEXT

Perhaps putting things in a global or historic context may help. In very recent UK history, and around the world at this very minute, very, very few people have had or have as much disposable income as you have now.

In the EU, 10 of the 27 countries have a minimum wage of less than 600 Euros a month (about £500/per month). World Bank research shows that, even today, 2 billion (2000,000,000) people live on £2 a day.

Feeling connected to other people by spending quality time with them, having fun, is completely free of charge. As is volunteering in your community. See *Quality time (Part 2, Chapter 11)* for ideas. Spending your time buying things you don't need, with money you don't have (levels of personal debt have been rising since 2016 in the UK) is bad both for the planet and your stress levels.

Ask yourself, what qualities do you admire in others? Kindness, modesty, humour, determination, a sense of duty, respect for others, loyalty, calm, integrity, willingness to learn new things, to develop as a person, to change? What qualities would you like to pass on to the next generation?

Are any of these likely to be inculcated through getting and spending? Or are they more likely to found and grown through playing sports, learning new skills, volunteering in your community, spending time in nature and connecting in ways that serve other people, other species, the Environment?

I leave you with a sobering thought. Slaves were once *branded* with hot iron and wore *chains*. Many of us give up our freedom from money worries to wear our *brands* of *chain* store labels. Who is your master? The *brand*ing consultants and the advertisers of *chain* stores - or you?

## Chapter 33

# From Frying Pan to Fire

People often rush out of, or give up on, a difficult relationship only to find themselves in a far worse situation, emotionally and financially.

This is particularly relevant where children are involved. If you separate from the other parent, you will exchange a romantic partnership for a co-parenting relationship with them which will endure until you both die. It will still involve negotiating with them to ensure your child(ren) have two parents to care for them, but without the levers you can pull if you live together. It will also probably involve your next partner feeling cheesed off by the demands your ex-partner/your children make on your new life as a couple together.

Is the grass really greener? It will certainly be *different* if you part company. But without either partner undergoing some serious self-examination or therapy, it rarely ends up more nutritious.

Before undertaking as major a change as separation/divorce, it might be worth examining your reasons to do so very carefully. It takes courage to call the other person out when their behaviour is sub-standard. It is easier to chip away at the other person with sarcastic or bitter remarks and/or be angry, resentful or passive-aggressive. That way, we don't have to risk the other person showing us that they don't care about our feelings.

Often we don't even know what our feelings are – just that the other person has cheesed us off. Putting into words the exact reason for the exact feeling we are experiencing is really hard work! Carping on at our partner for having shortcomings is much easier. After all, you get to order a main dish of one-up-man-ship followed by a delicious dessert of self-righteousness, as you send them to the dog house! But the problem is that you are only storing up bad feeling for the next time the whole sorry row repeats.

When we divorce, we don't necessarily divorce our partner in a psychological sense. We divorce the part of ourselves who has behaved in ways we didn't like. The problem is that we unconsciously turn our partners into marionettes so that they will behave in the ways we implicitly expect them too (eg. I expect my partner to be controlling the way my Dad controlled my Mum).

Then, when our partner turns out to be our willing marionette, we vilify them and divorce them. But the part of us that found a controlling partner wasn't *in* the partner alone, it was in *us*. And so without understanding our part in what went wrong, we will inevitably reproduce it.

Are we unhappy in our relationship because we are driven by *oughts*? Eg. *'I* ought *to feel in love with my partner and I don't'* or, *'My friend's relationship is better than mine because of X, Y or Z.'*

It might be foolish to give up prematurely. Identifying the symptoms which make our relationships ill is hard but profitable work. You cannot help what you feel - but you are in charge of what you *do* about those feelings.

Have you done some *Thinking (Part 1, Chapter 3)* about whether your *oughts* are reasonable, even achievable? If you conclude they are, have you examined your *Feelings* and *Expectations (Part 1, Chapters 2 & 4)* and identified what you may need to change as a priority and what can be left further down the list to get to, as and when your relationship can absorb more changes?

Use *The art of negotiation (Part 3, Chater 17)* to tackle each issue in turn that is causing you distress, then plan each conversation carefully. It might just enable you to implement the changes you need to make the relationship a happier place to live.

## QUESTIONS TO MULL OVER

- *Have I thought this through?*
- *Can I re-revaluate what I've got?*
- *What are the practical implications of losing this relationship?*
- *Could I put more effort into peacekeeping and rebuilding? If so, how?*

# CHAPTER 34

## ANGER WITH THE WORLD

The outside world can be a difficult place. But how you respond to it makes a critical difference as to whether it impacts on you and your family's health.

Imagine your partner and child are out for a walk. A barking dog alarms the child, but the dog is on a lead. Your partner gets angry with the owner for scaring the child and snatches the child away. This encourages irrational fear in the child (dogs on leads are perfectly safe) and reinforces the message that the child should be scared of the world as they rant on about dangerous dogs and how people shouldn't be allowed to have them...

The parent and child keep walking and a cyclist whizzes past quite close to them, riding on the pavement. The child didn't even notice the bike, the cyclist judged their distance/speed well and didn't hurt anyone. The child has no in-built notion that bikes are dangerous. But your partner is again angry about what *might* have happened. The actual cyclist is long gone so the parent turns their anger on to cyclists in general or how rubbish the Police are not to arrest them, or how badly the Council has devised the bike lane.

On their way home, they run into a rich neighbour just back from an exotic holiday who boasts about their fabulous trip. This person is not a physical threat but causes envy and/or resentment to fester inside your partner's breast.

The point here is that nothing bad has actually happened. The dog was no danger, the bike was no danger and the neighbour was quite friendly. Back at home, your partner, angry about all these potential threats, may spill out these imagined wrongs on to you, overheard by your child.

The best thing you can do for your partner in this situation is to stay calm. Make your home together a safe place. Don't reinforce imagined fears by sharing angry dog stories or amplifying their fears. Concentrate on trying to see that your partner's threatened state may well relate to how they came to see the world when they were young (a bad childhood) and/or how they learnt to see the world through the eyes of their own anxious parent.

Changing habits is hard but it can be done. See if you can get them to read *Improving self-esteem* and *Keeping calm (Part 1, Chapters 5 & 6)* for ideas on how.

CHAPTER 35

## COPING WITH TEENAGERS

- **The developing brain**
- **How to cope with it**

### THE DEVELOPING BRAIN

Put simply the human brain has older and newer parts. The older part, the limbic brain, is the bit we share with all our mammalian cousins and it operates pre-language. It reacts, instantly and emotionally, to any stimulus. Your brain is composed of 100 billion neurons and 10 times as many other cells which support those neurons. They all communicate via electrical and chemical signalling; this is often referred to as the 'wiring'.

Our distinctly human part of the brain is packed into our skull above our eyebrows. This area is far larger in us than in even our closest primate relatives, chimpanzees, with whom we share 98.8% of our DNA. Known as the prefrontal cortex, it is where we think from, talk from, plan from and inhibit our limbic responses from.

It develops in two bursts of activity. The first is from 0-3 years and it depends on good caregiving to develop well. This is why many people with traumatic starts may struggle to manage their anger, jealousy or sad feelings in later life. See *Emotions (Part 1, Chapter 1)*.

Your brain isn't fully 'wired' until you turn 25 years old and the prefrontal cortex in particular undergoes a huge amount of re-wiring between puberty and age 25. When you realise this, you can see the teenage years are a bit like trying to repair a jet engine while flying across the Atlantic! It is a wonder they can get themselves to school with the right books and their shoes on at all! So try to give your teenager the benefit of the doubt and have faith that they will cope OK as adults, if you can behave relatively kindly and calmly towards them most of the time, during these tricky years.

To see the limbic and prefrontal brain areas working in concert, think of a time when someone was *really* annoying you. Your limbic system fired and you felt rage, making you want to hit them. Then, hopefully, your prefrontal cortex inhibited that behaviour and you shouted at them instead, or even better stormed out of the room before you said anything really horrid!

Teenagers haven't got the two parts working together terribly well yet, so try to be forgiving of them where you can. If you find *yourself* being violent towards your teenager, please see the page on *Violence (Part 4, Chapter 27)*.

## How To Cope With It

Acknowledge to yourself (and them if they are listening) that their developing brain is a possible cause of difficult or unacceptable behaviours.

Accept that instant, emotion-based reactions are not under an adolescent's conscious control and can occur for plenty of other reasons besides you (stress from academic pressure, friendship issues, broken heart, hunger, tiredness, for example).

If they get angry with you, adopt the tactics set out in *Bad Reactions: Anger (Part 4, Chapter 22)*.

Above all keep calm. Listen. Be *seen* to be listening.

Ask them to express themselves as calmly as they can in saying what it is they want, or plan to do. Model calmness by repeating back to them what they have said using *their own words* in a non-challenging way. Say

---

'*OK. Have I got that right? Do you think we need to think about*…[list the consequences, one at a time]? Ask *How can we bring that about/make that happen?*'

---

The point of this technique is to turn angry, scared, confused animosity into a loving, joint exploration of possibilities. Once the anger is defused, even small changes may satisfy both parties.

For teenagers, the question of *Where do I fit in?* is a massive preoccupation. They are having to give up the safety of being a child in their nuclear family to stand on their own two feet in the world and they desperately need the approval of their peers to manage this feat. This is why they are so upset if you are seen to be clipping their wings and making them look 'uncool'. It is also why you only need to *breathe* for them to see you as embarrassing!

But paradoxically, they also need you to lay down solid boundaries for them, so they don't feel too overwhelmed by the crazier demands of their peers. So stick to what you think is reasonable, but be reasonable in *how* you do it and they will thank you (one day!)

Remember you are walking a tightrope between keeping them safe on the one hand and wanting to have the control like you did when they were little. So ask yourself which side of the rope you are talking from and make sure it is the safety side and not your controlling side.

All normal children sooner or later move their bodies and minds away from parental comfort and control. Be prepared to keep giving but expect less in return. Expect them to be selfish and self-absorbed from age 12 to 20!

As to *your* feelings, well I am sorry to say they are 100% your responsibility, whatever the teenage provocation! Regret, fear, anger, blame, self-pity, feeling unwanted - these are all justifiable feelings which you must work through - as you face the reality that time moves on and you can't stop the bird flying the nest. (For a nice poem about this, see Kahlil Gibran's *Talk to us of children*).

Your child *may* occasionally feel compassion for your position and if you are doing well enough, they will keep sharing things, in ways compatible with their changing life stages. But this will *not* necessarily sync up with your expectations! It is worth re-reading *Feelings (Part 1, Chapter 2)* to help you cope with the painful work of parenting a teenager.

Lastly, I have found it helpful to remember that when you feel like the servant of your teenager, you should remember they are the **servant of *your* genes**!

For more on the science of teenage brains, see Teenage Brains in *Other Resources (Part 6)*.

## CHAPTER 36

# COPING WITH STEP-CHILDREN

Question: What can this little book add to the dozens of parenting websites and lawyers online, all of which have something wise to say?

Answer? Essential skills.

- **Critical thinking**
- **Warm-up techniques**
- **Communication skills**
- **Negotiation**

## CRITICAL THINKING

Your new step-family, by definition, can't and won't be perfect. In that regard, it exactly resembles a 'normal' family which is never perfect either! So every time you feel furious about something, ask yourself, *'Will what is bothering me, still be bothering me on my death bed?'* It can take five years and maybe longer to make a reconstituted step-family work and during that time you should expect many dysfunctional moments.

Don't raise the bar too high and definitely keep it *very* low if you are coming together during the adolescence of any children in your new family. See *Coping with teenagers (Part 5, Chapter 35)* for more on this challenge.

Ask yourself, what is it you really want to change, either about your partner's attitude to their children, the children themselves or their/your attitude to their ex-partner? Essentially, what do you really want?

What might the others in the family picture really want? Can you analyse the practical considerations to understand the emotions driving them? What does each person in the family really want, especially at an emotional level?

What can you/they do differently to deliver their/your demands? If the price feels high for you or for them, is there something you/they might be willing to trade for it?

## WARM-UP TECHNIQUES

You wouldn't run a race or sing a song without warming up.

The idea that you can decide, communicate and negotiate about high-stakes, long-term issues without warm-ups and preparation is a sad folly. Have a read of *Learning to listen* (Part 2, Chapter 13) and *Get your partner talking* (Part 3, Chapter 18) before you start. Then use *The art of negotiation (Part 3, Chapters 17)* to prepare for a difficult conversation.

## COMMUNICATION SKILLS

What words to use, when, how to say them?

Psychologists and advertisers know how to get their message across. Most of us, especially in the home, sadly don't. We speak in ways we would never dream of doing at work or at school. Then we are surprised that the results are poor! See sections on *Keeping calm (Part 1, Chapter 6), Communicating well (Part 2, Chapter 12)* and *Asking the right questions (Part 3, Chapter 15)* for more on this.

## Negotiation

Whether you are dealing with a step-child, your partner, your ex- or their ex-, the chances are you want changes to the current set-up. First off, remember that all negotiation involves give and take.

You have to find something the other wants, or thinks is fair to trade. People inevitably value different things. One of the big secrets in negotiations is never to use blame words. The past is the past. You need new plans to look ahead.

As you gain more skills, problems can be better understood and tackled constructively. See *Finding the middle ground (Part 3, Chapter 16)* for more on this.

## Be the change you want to see

Lots of websites can tell you how the law works in divorce and how step-parents can gain more parental rights, but none tell you how to gain the co-operation of an ex-partner or how to broker peace between all the parties concerned.

This book does teach those skills. Practice them and you will model for your children and step-children skills that will serve them well for every relationship they will go on to have in life, be it with a teacher, employer, partner or their own children. *Remember, children do what we do, not what we say!*

# PART SIX

## NEXT STEPS

# CHAPTER 37

## THE WORKSHOP

This part of the book uses the least possible words.

All the reading you have done in this book needs reinforcement by action and practice. These exercises can be done alone, with a real friend or hopefully, with your partner.

Here are things *to do* to turn this book's ideas into your habits:

**Cherish** your partner - a touch, a kind word, a compliment, some praise, some thanks.

**Develop** your 5 senses - little things control the mood, so set the scene.

- **Smell** essential oils, coffee, cooking, baking, flowers. Whatever you and your partner both enjoy.
- **Touch** warms and calms. A teddy bear, a string of pearls, a soft scarf.
- **Hear** well-chosen music is better for mood and stress than TV chatter.

- **Taste** a tiny touch of quality chocolate, nougat, olive oil, a good cheese, a fine port or sherry. They don't go off, so small savourings are possible.
- **See** books, art books, magazines, fabrics - all offer instant pleasure if well chosen. Even the colours and shapes of supper on the plate contribute to the mood.

**Understand** your partner. He/she is not an unchanging statue. He/she has urges, drives, hopes, fears, worries, ambitions, attitudes, assumptions, plans, issues about work, the people at work, money, health, body image, ageing, expectations. Unfortunately many of us inherited our notions of loving and being loved at a deep emotional level from our parents. Although painful and sometimes tearful, you do need to explore his/her childhood memories - happy, sad and scary. All the evidence, and there's lots of it, shows that couples who share more, bond better, and stick together.

**Listen** to them. Look at, nod, touch, laugh with (not at) them, use your body posture to communicate interest. Do not fidget, sigh with boredom, look elsewhere when they are engaging you in conversation.

**Communicate with words**. Frankly this is hard. People wrongly assume that there is just one normal, natural, neutral way to say everyday words. There isn't. Prove this to yourself by imagining that you are using the word "sorry". Say it as if you were apologising to a child for dropping their ice cream. Now to your mother when you are furious with her. Now to a friend you know you have done a wrong to but you feel really guilty about it. Now to your boss for letting down the team. Now to someone who you just bumped into with your supermarket trolley. All different, right?

**You** regularly say words kindly, patiently, enquiringly, impatiently, dismissively, angrily, even contemptuously.

**Record** in writing a dozen everyday phrases that you use, at work, at home, in shops. Then on your own with a mirror or to your phone, record you saying your common phrases in the different ways listed above. *Remember: If you are not in control of your tone, your emotions will be and they can sabotage your intentions and therefore the success of your communications.*

**Communicate through body language.** Words carry only half the message. Your tone, face, body language all matter. Humans learned to read signs and signals long before we learned speech. Be aware. Use a big mirror. Give yourself choices.

**Disagreements/Arguments/Middle Ground.** We cannot avoid disagreeing with our partner. But we can learn to assume *we* are not right in every detail and to question our assumption that disagreeing with us makes our partner either stupid or bad! In any fight, separate what is relevant to the relationship right now from all the other stuff that people bicker about, from whose football team is better to whom to vote into power.

If an issue is just about a difference of opinion with few consequences, let it go. If it is a bigger issue for you, use the phrases below to keep tempers under control:

---

*"Interesting…but I'm not sure I fully understand the detail, please go on."*

---

> *"OK if that's right, how would it effect...X* [allow pause for thought], *or Y* (pause)."

The most certain of shouters often defeats him/herself when faced calmly and coolly with detailed implications. If there are unbridgeable differences, try:

> *"OK, you want to do/change X. I understand."* (Let that sink in).

> *"If so, do you mind if I do/change Y?"*

Don't shout, stamp, weep. Keep calm. Assume there may be some good in his/her position. If the disagreements are about **power** (not uncommon) a little humour can ease things:

> *"Ok, I see that you want to be the boss and decide things. But I too need to be the boss on some issues so let's make a list of where you can be boss and where I can be boss and then we can work through the issues on which we must agree."*

**You communicating with you.** With pen and paper write down in a list all your good points and strengths. Praise yourself. Next write a list of the thoughts, attitudes, skills, behaviours you *need* to improve and then those you'd *like* to improve.

**Quiz time.** You will now have some ideas about your **ideal** self and three questions must be addressed:

1. Where did your expectations come from? Parents, siblings, television, social media, neighbours, work mates? Please write down the detail, slow writing aids thinking.
2. Given the realities of your life, how realistic is it to compare yourself with these role models? Write reasons for comparisons.
3. What's stopping you? What inner voices are giving you unhelpful messages?

Here's a **fun** game. Imagine someone has given you a really gloomy parrot. The parrot has been trained to repeat defeatist parrot talk. *"That's too difficult"*, *"That won't work" etc.* Every time a negative thought crops up in your own mind simply *shout at the parrot* rather than take the gloom seriously.

## POSITIVE REINFORCEMENT

Psychologists don't know why this works but it does. Register another email address so you can email yourself. Make a list of very short simple messages relevant to *your* situation. Send the emails to yourself.

**Paradox.** You know that you have sent the messages but there is something in the ritual of it that wriggles into our brains. The phrases you send must address your issues but here are some ideas:

- *We can make it work.*
- *There is more good than bad.*
- *I love his/her touch/smile/jokes (make it specific to your partner).*
- *We've both changed because we have grown apart, but that means we can grow back towards each other by doing shared activities and spending quality time together.*

# CHAPTER 38

# BEFORE SEEKING PROFESSIONAL HELP

Despite the plethora of relationship advice out there (see *Other Resources, Part 6*), according to Relate, you are not alone: some 6 million couples in the UK alone are struggling.

If you have tried, tried and tried again to communicate in a kind and calm way using the suggestions in this book, but are still finding things are really stuck, it might be time to seek some professional help.

Simplify the therapist's task by probing the situation from some different perspectives.

- **Cultural Norms**
- **Role Models**
- **Choice**
- **Expectations**

## CULTURAL NORMS

Modern Western society is very big on promoting individual rights and individual greed. Consumerist culture promotes an 'I' not a 'We' agenda. It wants us to work, borrow and buy. Sharing and caring doesn't make money, so corporations have no investment in promoting it widely. In what ways could you counter that pull by considering how to develop the following values in your relationship?

- **understanding**
- **compassion**
- **tolerance**
- **forgiveness**

## ROLE MODELS

It must be said that there's more bad behaviour on TV and social media than tenderness. The media is where we unconsciously absorb our culture's attitudes and vocabulary. Who are your role models for a relationship? Who do you hold in high esteem as a couple that you actually *know*? Can you identify not just the 'way' those couples are together, but what particular actions they engage in which you could try doing too? Would it be possible to engage them in a dialogue about your difficulties and see what advice they could offer?

## CHOICE

With so much more choice as to how to spend our time and money, it isn't surprising that couples can just grow apart, with different interests or intense pressure on time due to work constraints/demands of raising children. Successful relationships often revolve around shared interests. If you don't have any shared interests, could you start to develop some? What new leisure activities could you take up together?

## EXPECTATIONS

When first in love, few couples ask, *Where do we want this to go?* so it's not surprising when they end up wanting different things, especially if they don't have open communication channels. Are you unhappy because you are comparing your life/relationship to other people? On what are you basing your assumptions about these 'happier' people? If it is Facebook/Instagram, then remember how distorting of reality social media platforms really are. Pictures lie. Smiles belie heartache. Nothing on social media is what it seems.

# CHAPTER 39

# OTHER RESOURCES

- **Learning more**
- **Seeking Professional help**

## LEARNING MORE

### Attachment theory

**Very Well Mind** - what is attachment theory?
*www.verywellmind.com/what-is-attachment-theory-2795337*

**Annie Pesskin's blog** - how attachment patterns shape your relationships
*psychoanalysisinotherstories.com/2019/01/21/pull-yourself-together*

### Brains keep changing

**Brain Pickings blog** - Carol Dweck's theory of the Growth vs. Fixed mindset
*www.brainpickings.org/2014/01/29/carol-dweck-mindset*

**MindSetHealth** - how to develop a growth mindset
*www.mindsethealth.com/matter/growth-vs-fixed-mindset#toc-who-identified-the-growth-mindset--2*

**Annie Pesskin's blog** - how the mind is a prediction machine
*psychoanalysisinotherstories.com/2021/02/08/the-loom-of-origins*

**TED talk** - your unconscious brain in action
*www.youtube.com/watch?v=NilvW_ACG9M&t=785s*

Cognitive bias

**Wikipedia** - list of cognitive biases
*en.wikipedia.org/wiki/Cognitive_bias#List_of_biases*

**The Decision Lab** - Daniel Kahneman (Nobel prize winner)'s useful resource
*thedecisionlab.com*

Choice confuses

**TED Talk: Barry Schwartz** - how choice confuses
*www.ted.com/talks/barry_schwartz_the_paradox_of_choice?language=en*

Difficult behaviours

**KSL Training.com** - coping with difficult customers
*www.ksl-training.co.uk/free-resources/customer-service/dealing-with-difficult-behaviour*

**Psyche Magazine** - saving a relationship on the brink
*psyche.co/guides/how-to-save-a-romantic-relationship-thats-on-the-brink*

**UK Trauma Council** - spotting behaviours caused by trauma
*uktraumacouncil.org*

<u>Emotions</u>

**Technology Review.com** - why feelings matter
*www.technologyreview.com/2014/06/17/172310/the-importance-of-feelings*

**Wikipedia -** emotions
*en.wikipedia.org/wiki/Emotion*

**Joanne Davila's TED talk** - developing romantic competency
*singjupost.com/joanne-davila-skills-for-healthy-romantic-relationships-at-tedxsbu-transcript/?singlepage=1t*

<u>Framing</u>

**Short Form.com** - how framing works
*www.shortform.com/blog/framing-effect-definition-examples*

<u>Keeping Calm</u>

**YouTube** - isometric exercises
*www.youtube.com/results?search_query=isometric+exercises*

**YouTube** - Tai Chi exercises
*www.youtube.com/results?search_query=tai+chi*

**Do Yoga With Me.com** - free online yoga and meditation classes
*www.doyogawithme.com*

**Dr. Dan Siegel.com** - SIFTing techniques
*www.drdansiegel.com*

## Laughter

**Psychology Today** - why play matters
*www.psychologytoday.com/gb/blog/animal-emotions/201405/the-importance-play-having-fun-must-be-taken-seriously*

**Pressmen, S. (2009)** - how fun generates wellbeing
*pubmed.ncbi.nlm.nih.gov/19592515*

## Making your face match your message

**Woodson, B.** - 30 emotions to practice
*www.youtube.com/watch?v=y2YUMPJATmg*

**Rao, R.** - the same phrase in 15 ways
*www.youtube.com/watch?v=Fh2ouhh0ITw&list=RDtiicx0d7yBg&index=2*

**Male Faces** - photos of emotions
*www.researchgate.net/figure/a-Example-prototypical-expressions-of-six-basic-emotions*

**Teenage Girls** - photos of emotions
*www.shutterstock.com/image-photo/teenager-girl-different-facial-expression-face-71395306*

**Older Female Faces** - photos of emotions
*www.shutterstock.com/search/older+woman+facial+expressions*

Negotiation skills

**Skills You Need.com** - developing negotiation skills
*www.skillsyouneed.com/ips/negotiation.html*

Questioning techniques

**Nielsen Norman Group** - asking open-ended questions
*www.nngroup.com/articles/open-ended-questions*

Parenting

**Winnicott, D.** - 18 reasons why you might resent your baby
*www.ncbi.nlm.nih.gov/pmc/articles/PMC3330380*

Relationships and why they matter

**Harvard Study of Adult Development** - genes help but
joy is better
*www.adultdevelopmentstudy.org*

Alcohol/Substance Issues

**Alcoholics Anonymous** - support for alcoholics
*www.alcoholics-anonymous.org.uk*

**Al Anon** - support for those in relationships with people
suffering addiction issues
*al-anonuk.org.uk/*

**Web MD.com** - addiction treatment options
*www.webmd.com/connect-to-care/addiction-treatment-recovery/porn-addiction-treatments*

## Teenage Brains

**Science Daily.com** - brains keep developing until 25
*www.sciencedaily.com/releases/2011/09/110922134617.htm*

**Raising Children.net** - teenage brain development
*raisingchildren.net.au/pre-teens/development/understanding-your-pre-teen/brain-development-teens#teenage-brain-development-the-basics-nav-title*

**Parent and Teen.com** - how teenagers make decisions
*parentandteen.com/how-teens-make-decisions*

**Stanford Childrens.org** - judgement in teenage brains
*www.stanfordchildrens.org/en/topic/default?id=understanding-the-teen-brain-1-3051*

# SEEKING PROFESSIONAL HELP

## Online Personal Development Courses

**https://ecourse.psychalive.org** - with Dr. Lisa Firestone and Dr. Daniel Siegel
*ecourse.psychalive.org*

## Physical Abuse and/or Violence

**UK Government** - domestic abuse advice
*www.gov.uk/guidance/domestic-abuse-how-to-get-help*

**Women's Aid** - support and advice for women
*www.womensaid.org.uk/information-support*

**Citizens Advice Bureau** - gender violence
*www.citizensadvice.org.uk/family/gender-violence/domestic-violence-and-abuse-getting-help*

**National Domestic Abuse Helpline** - 0808 2000 247
*www.nationaldahelpline.org.uk*

**Who's in Charge Helpline?** - 07814 378 325/07966 592 632
*whosincharge.co.uk*

**Family Lives Helpline** - 0808 800 2222
*www.familylives.org.uk*

**Muslim Womens' Network** - domestic abuse helpline
*www.mwnhelpline.co.uk/issuesstep2.php?id=14*

**The Change Project** - helping abusers change
*www.thechange-project.org*

Couples Counselling or Personal Therapy

**British Psychoanalytic Council** - psychodynamic psychotherapy register
*www.bpc.org.uk/information-support/find-a-therapist-or-clinic*

**British Association of Counselling and Psychotherapy** - register of practitioners
*www.bacp.co.uk*

**UK Council for Psychotherapy** - register of practitioners
*www.psychotherapy.org.uk*

**Relate** - couple counselling
*www.relate.org.uk*

Sexual problems

**Relate** - sexual problems
*www.relate.org.uk/relationship-help/help-sex/sex-common-problems/
weve-stopped-having-sex*

**Relate** - sex therapy
*www.relate.org.uk/relationship-help/help-sex/sex-therapy*

**Esther Perel** - brilliant U.S. couple therapist with podcast
and blogs
*www.estherperel.com*

Printed in Great Britain
by Amazon